The Emerging Markets
of the Middle East

The Emerging Markets of the Middle East

Strategies for Entry and Growth

Tim J. Rogmans

First published in 2012 by
Business Expert Press, LLC
222 East 46th Street, New York, NY 10017
www.businessexpertpress.com

ISBN-13: 978-1-60649-205-5 (paperback)

ISBN-13: 978-1-60649-206-2 (e-book)

DOI 10.4128/9781606492062

Business Expert Press International Business collection

Collection ISSN: 1948-2752 (print)
Collection ISSN: 1948-2760 (electronic)

Cover design by Jonathan Pennell
Interior design by Exeter Premedia Services Private Ltd.,
Chennai, India

First edition: 2012

10 9 8 7 6 5 4 3 2 1

Printed in the United States of America.

To Dani and Yasmina

Abstract

The Emerging Markets of the Middle East: Strategies for Entry and Growth is aimed at managers who are planning growth strategies for Middle Eastern markets, either as newcomers into the region or on the basis of an existing operation in one or several Middle Eastern countries.

Over the next decade, the economies of the Middle East will continue to be characterized by rapid growth, political turmoil, and increasing competitive intensity. International investors have the choice either to ignore the region all together and bypass business opportunities with great potential or to make a careful assessment of which countries to enter and how to enter them successfully. This book is the first of its kind to include the information, insights, and frameworks that are required to develop entry and growth strategies for the Middle East in the new turbulent environment following the global economic crisis and the Arab Spring.

The first part of this book provides an in-depth analysis of the major developments that determines the business environment of different countries in the region. This section includes a discussion of major social and economic developments, the impact of the rise of multinational companies from the Middle East, and the role played by institutions and political risk.

The second part deals with each of the major decisions that a company planning to grow in the region needs to make: Which countries to enter? What is the right entry mode and ownership structure? How to choose between a greenfield operation and an acquisition? This book concludes with practical advice on the process of setting up operations in the Middle East.

Keywords

Middle East, emerging markets, entry strategies, foreign direct investment, institutions, multinationals, political risk, Arab Spring

Contents

Preface ix

Chapter 1   Emerging Middle East 1

Part 1   The Emerging Markets of the Middle East................. **11**

Chapter 2   Middle East Megatrends 13

Chapter 3   The Rise of Multinational Companies from
the Middle East 33

Chapter 4   Institutions and Risk...45

Part 2   Strategies for Entry and Growth **59**

Chapter 5   Location Choices...61

Chapter 6   Entry and Operation Modes..............................71

Chapter 7   Mergers and Acquisitions..................................85

Chapter 8   Implementation Considerations.........................97

Appendix: Country Profiles..105

Notes..113

References 117

Useful Websites 121

About the Author...123

Index 125

Preface

The Emerging Markets of the Middle East: Strategies for Entry and Growth is aimed at managers who are planning growth strategies for Middle Eastern markets, either as newcomers into the region or on the basis of an existing operation in one or several Middle Eastern countries.

Over the next decade, the economies of the Middle East will continue to be characterized by rapid growth, political turmoil, and increasing competitive intensity. International investors have the choice either to ignore the region all together and bypass business opportunities with great potential or to make a careful assessment of which countries to enter and how to enter them successfully. This book is the first of its kind to include the information, insights, and frameworks that are required to develop entry and growth strategies for the Middle East in the new turbulent environment following the global economic crisis and the Arab Spring. In this new context, companies that have not yet entered the region are asking themselves what opportunities exist and how to capitalize on them. Existing players are also now in the process of redefining their regional plans after a period of rapid growth, sudden slowdown, and gradual recovery.

The first part of this book provides an in-depth analysis of the major developments that determines the business environment of different countries in the region. This section includes a discussion of major social and economic developments, the impact of the rise of multinational companies from the Middle East, and the role played by institutions and political risk. In this context, this book intends to clarify both what makes the countries in the region similar and what makes them very different from each other.

The second part deals with each of the major decisions that a company planning to grow in the region needs to make: Which countries to enter? What is the right entry mode and ownership structure? How to choose between a greenfield operation and an acquisition? This book concludes with practical advice on the process of setting up operations in the Middle East.

The aim of this book is to provide support for executives who need to make strategic decisions that are in reality often based on personal preferences of key personnel or result from specific opportunities that arise. Although the role of these more opportunistic elements in the business planning process is undeniable and highly relevant, this book serves as a guide to put all potential opportunities into perspective and to make the right decisions quickly in a structured manner.

CHAPTER 1

Emerging Middle East

Multinational companies cannot afford to ignore emerging markets.
Nor can they afford to ignore the difficulties involved.[1]
                                        —*Financial Times*, August 14, 2011

Since the global economic slowdown that started in 2008, businesses
have increasingly looked at the world's rapidly developing economies as
a source of profitable growth. Today, the vast majority of the business
literature on emerging markets has a strong focus on the major economies of Asia and Latin America, particularly the BRIC countries (Brazil,
Russia, India and China) and sometimes other large economies such as
Indonesia, South Africa and Turkey. The countries of the Middle East
are usually not included in these discussions, despite displaying many of
the key characteristics of emerging markets, including strong economic
growth, growing populations and rapid institutional development coupled with ongoing political instability. The lack of attention to the Middle
East may be due to the fragmentation of the region into a number of
smaller markets, none of which can compete in size with any of the BRIC
nations. It may also be because the Middle East is often perceived as a
risky and difficult market to operate in, especially among investors with
no direct experience in the region. The dramatic changes that started with
the Arab Spring have made it tempting for multinational companies to
put Middle East expansion plans on the back burner. This attitude is
understandable given the difficulties many companies have faced in raising finance since 2008 and the apparently larger and easier to capture
opportunities in other emerging markets. However, ignoring the growth
potential of the Middle East would be a mistake for any company with
global ambitions. Indeed, many companies have successfully entered the
region over the last two decades and have enjoyed rapid and profitable
growth, as well as challenges on the way.

Today, business in the Middle East is once again at a crossroads. The companies that have already established operations are reviewing their strategies in light of the new economic and political realities. On the other hand, companies whose emerging market strategy has until now focused on the BRIC nations are considering how to capitalize on opportunities in the Middle East. This book aims to be a guide for managers designing and implementing business strategies for the Middle East. Based on seven years of research, consulting and training experience in the region, the book provides information, insights, mini-cases and frameworks to help companies design a path to profitable growth.

Are the Middle East Economies *Emerging Markets?*

The term *emerging markets* was coined by Antoine van Agtmael in 1981 while working at the International Finance Corporation.[2] Although there is still no generally accepted definition of the term, two features of emerging markets stand out. First, emerging markets are characterized by rapid growth. This growth is usually expressed in terms of income levels and population, but may also include other elements such as infrastructure and education levels. Emerging markets usually start from a lower base than developed markets in terms of per capita Gross Domestic Product (GDP) and are in a process of catching up. In terms of economic growth, the Middle East on the whole has definitely grown faster than the more developed markets of Europe and the United States during the past decade. Oil-rich Middle Eastern countries such as Kuwait, Qatar and the United Arab Emirates (UAE) already have per capita income levels that are at least on a par with developed countries and can perhaps no longer be called emerging markets according to income levels. It is a paradox that Qatar and the UAE, countries that rank among the richest in the world in terms of GDP per capita and are still growing relatively quickly, have been struggling to get their stock markets upgraded from *frontier* to *emerging market* status by Morgan Stanley Capital International.

This paradox is due to another key feature of emerging markets, which is that these countries are still developing, particularly with respect to institutions that help to facilitate business transactions. A recent book on *Winning in Emerging Markets*[3] refers to these developments in progress as *institutional voids*. The imperfections in the institutional infrastructure of an emerging market can take various forms, ranging from inadequate physical and human infrastructure to ineffective commercial legislation. According to this view of emerging markets, even developed countries are still emerging in some ways, as no country is ever *fully developed*. In terms of institutional development, emerging markets are somewhere between the so-called failed states and the Western economies and many of these emerging economies are catching up fast. The opening up of markets to foreign competition and the growing membership of organizations such as the World Trade Organization (WTO) are helping to create a rule-based framework for doing business around the world, thereby improving the institutional framework in emerging markets. For example, Saudi Arabia's entry into the WTO in 2005 was accompanied by a massive jump in Foreign Direct Investment (FDI). As Saudi Arabia adapted its commercial legislation and started to promote FDI, it became an interesting market for a growing number of multinational companies.

Institutional voids are an impediment to doing business in emerging markets but they offer important business opportunities as well. As imperfections exist in the markets for products, labor and capital, suppliers with appropriate assets and skills can profit from helping countries to fill the relevant gaps. For example, imperfections in capital markets may make it difficult to assess the credit worthiness of borrowers, but this market imperfection provides business opportunities for private equity companies, credit information providers and financial training companies.

There can be little doubt that countries in the Middle East can be classified as emerging markets. However, the region is very different from the other emerging markets of Asia and Latin America and there are also many differences between countries within the region. With roughly half of the world's GDP and more than half of the world's economic growth coming from emerging markets, it is no longer appropriate to speak of *emerging market strategies*, except at the highest, most general, level. Such high-level strategies need to be complemented with regional and country-level strategies in order to become operational.

The scope of this book includes the Arab Middle East, a region consisting of 13 countries and 200 million people. Table 1.1 provides an overview of the key characteristics of these Middle Eastern economies.

Table 1.1. Overview of Arab Middle East Countries (2010)

	Population (million)	GDP ($ in billions)	GDP per capita ($)	Average annual real GDP growth % (2007–2011)
Bahrain	1.3	22.7	20,475	4.8
Egypt	80.4	218.5	2,789	5.2
Iraq	31.5	82.5	2,619	5.2
Jordan	6.5	27.5	4,500	5.1
Kuwait	3.1	131.3	36,412	3.2
Lebanon	4.3	39.2	10,044	6.8
Oman	3.1	55.6	18,657	5.8
Palestinian Terr.	4.0	5.8	1,367	n/a
Qatar	1.7	129.5	76,168	16.6
Saudi Arabia	29.2	443.7	16,996	3.5
Syria	23.6	59.3	2,877	4.9*
UAE	5.4	301.9	59,717	2.9
Yemen	23.6	31.3	1,282	1.6

Sources: Population Reference Bureau,[3] United Nations Statistics Division,[4] International Monetary Fund.[5]
*Syria's GDP growth is for the period 2007–2010.

The region is characterized by growth along several important dimensions. First, the Middle East has the world's most rapidly growing population after Africa. Over the next 40 years, 175 million people will be added to the population of the countries covered in this book, representing an 81% increase over today's population. Economic growth has been strong, averaging an estimated 4.7% per annum during the period 2005–2010. In the same period, the total stock of FDI has grown by approximately tenfold and annual FDI inflows have increased from

$3.7 billion in 2000 to $55.3 billion in 2010. FDI inflows into the Middle East were even higher in 2008, when they peaked at $81.5 billion. The region now also boasts its fair share of emerging market multinationals, with companies such as Aramex, Emaar, Emirates Airlines, Orascom and SABIC making significant inroads into emerging and developed markets alike. The drivers of growth in the region will be discussed further in Chapter 2.

As true emerging markets, the economies of the Middle East cannot be characterized by growth alone. There are also significant institutional voids which are accompanied by great economic, social and political challenges. Although massive strides have been made in the development of the region's physical and human infrastructure, much remains to be done. The political turmoil that started in 2010 leaves a big question mark over the state of institutions in a number of countries. Successful companies in the Middle East will be aware of the institutional challenges they face and can exploit the business opportunities that arise from them.

Given the size and characteristics of the economies of the Arab Middle East, it is remarkable that most books on emerging markets largely ignore the Middle East. Khanna and Krishna in their recent book *Winning in Emerging Markets: A Roadmap for Strategy and Execution*[6] mention just one company from the Arab Middle East in the entire book, a description of the Kuwait-based Zain's entry into the African telecoms market. Antoine van Agtmael's *The Emerging Markets Century*[7] makes no mention at all of any Arab Middle Eastern country and none of the *world class multinationals* described in the book originate from the region. In reality, as will be demonstrated in Chapter 3, the region already boasts a number of world class multinationals who are having a global impact in their respective industries. Various other books similarly focus on the four BRIC countries and may make some mention of the *Next Eleven*,[8] a grouping of 11 large emerging markets, but pay very little attention to the Middle East. Today, the Middle East is economically significant and unique enough to warrant its own treatment in the business literature and in the strategic plans of multinational companies.

Scope and Outline of This Book

This book considers the Middle East from the perspective of companies looking to develop their business in the region. Doing business in this context may include manufacturing, marketing products and services, or making financial investments. The main objective is to serve as a guide for company executives looking to design or re-assess their strategic plans for the region. The book may be used on its own by business practitioners or as a guide for executive education programs.

The text is divided into two main parts. The first part deals with the business environment, including chapters on the most important developments that affect the business environment (Chapter 2), the rise of multinational corporations from the Middle East (Chapter 3), as well as institutions and risk (Chapter 4).

The second part provides guidance to investing companies with respect to their most important strategic choices. Chapter 5 deals with location choices, both for regional headquarters and for the establishment of country-level operations. Chapter 6 covers the entry mode and operation mode options available to investors. The terms entry and operation mode refer to various ownership structures that international companies may operate under, such as full ownership, joint ventures, franchising, licensing, or exports. Chapter 7 deals with establishment modes, referring to the question of *how* companies achieve their operation modes. The focus of this chapter is on mergers and acquisitions as a way of entering the Middle East. Chapter 8 concludes with the challenges of implementation and offers practical advice for foreign direct investors. The appendix contains a profile of each country covered in the book.

In practice, decisions on location choices, operation modes and establishment modes are not taken in a sequential way but are the result of an iterative process which is at least to some extent driven by the specific opportunities that are available to an investor. For example, a company may enter the region as a result of an attractive acquisition opportunity being presented and thereby decide on location and operation mode options without further specific consideration. Similarly, an investor may decide not to enter a certain market if the investor is unable to find a suitable distribution partner. The decision-making process is shown in Figure 1.1.

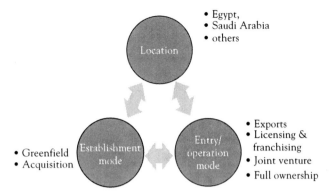

Figure 1.1. Strategic entry choices.

Intraregional Variations

Throughout this book, it is important to recognize that countries in the Middle East share important similarities but that there are also many differences between them. As can be seen from Table 1.1, countries in the region display a huge variety in terms of size, income and natural resource endowments. Egypt boasts a population of over 80 million, whereas Bahrain only has around 1 million people. Qatar has a GDP per capita of $76,168, among the highest in the world, while Yemen ranks among the world's poorer countries with a GDP per capita of only $1,282. Energy resource endowments are a major factor differentiating countries from each other, with the five Organization of the Petroleum Exporting Countries' (OPEC) members in the region controlling 45% of the world's proven oil reserves. As a result of these similarities and differences between countries, companies need both a regional and a local strategy, with the local strategy defined at the level of a country or even at the city level in the case of some of the larger or more diverse markets (e.g., Saudi Arabia, UAE, Egypt). Accordingly, this book will deal with the Middle East as one region *and* it will highlight the important differences between countries throughout the text whenever relevant from a strategy formulation perspective.

There are different ways of grouping countries together within the Middle East. One regional grouping that will be frequently referred to is that of the Gulf Cooperation Council (GCC) countries, consisting of

Bahrain, Kuwait, Oman, Qatar, Saudi Arabia and the UAE. These countries have important political, cultural and economic similarities. Each GCC country's economy benefits from the presence of energy resources, although Oman and Bahrain have much smaller energy reserves than the other GCC countries. The GCC countries have embarked on a process of economic integration, with the development of a common market. Plans for a common currency have been shelved for the time being, but right now there is very little currency risk between the countries of the GCC as each country has pegged its currency to either the dollar or a basket of currencies of which the dollar is an important component. The Arab Spring and tensions with Iran have given an increased political dimension to the GCC. In 2011, discussions started with Morocco and Jordan regarding their entry into the organization but there is no timetable for their accession as yet. In 2012, Saudi Arabia's proposal for further integration between the GCC states was adopted by the Council members.

Another, more loosely defined, region within the Middle East is the Levant which is generally understood to include those countries bordering the Eastern Mediterranean plus Jordan. For the Levant, the similarities between the countries are more cultural and historic rather than economic or political. There are no significant Levant-level government bodies or intergovernmental meetings or economic treaties.

Some analysts add North Africa to the definition of the region and define the Middle East North Africa (MENA) as their unit of analysis. The text contains some references to the MENA where it is not possible or practical to split out just the Middle East countries.

At this stage, it is worth pointing out what is not covered. First, the book does not go into detail about cultural differences and how to manage them, although some cultural issues are highlighted at relevant points throughout the text. The Arab Middle East is culturally too diverse to write about in general terms. In any case, the ways to recognize, respect and manage any cultural differences will largely depend on the cultural origin of the reader. Interested readers can easily find books on business etiquette and other cultural aspects of doing business in various Middle Eastern countries (see Appendix), although a decent website and conversations with people who have experience in the country in question (both locals and foreigners) can be an equally valuable starting point. Second, the book does not provide advice on how to adapt or maintain product and service designs for regional markets. Such considerations depend on many factors, including the market to be entered, the state of competition, the product or service under consideration and the investor's global strategic considerations. Investors are advised to carry out their own market research and speak to existing customers as well as prospects about these issues.

The Opportunity

The Middle East represents a large and rapidly growing market, strategically located at the crossroads between Asia, Europe and Africa and home to vast reserves of oil and gas. Immediately adjacent to the Arab Middle East, Turkey, India and Iran are other huge emerging markets which, given their size and unique characteristics, merit consideration in their own right and are not covered in detail here. However, their growth, as well as their challenges, provides great opportunities for the Middle East as a supplier and hub for the wider region. All these characteristics underpin the huge business potential offered by the Middle East.

The region is experiencing a high level of political turmoil which will affect business in a number of ways that are difficult to predict with accuracy. Visions about what the Middle East will look like in a decade from now have rarely been more divergent as they are today, ranging from democratic market-driven economies to autocratic theocracies. In all likelihood, political risk will remain at relatively high levels for the foreseeable future, with none of the more extreme scenarios being realized anytime soon. As a result, companies will need to accept environmental risk rather than expect it to disappear. Investors waiting for the dust to settle will be overtaken by companies that are more comfortable with uncertainty in the face of high potential returns. This book is intended to take at least some of the uncertainty away and give investors who are new to the region the confidence and the tools needed for successful business growth.

Companies who have already been operating in the Middle East over the last decade have experienced a rollercoaster ride consisting of a boom, a downturn and now a gradual recovery in those countries that are not heavily affected by political turmoil. During the downturn, many companies resorted to drastic cost cutting and opportunity hunting across the region as traditionally easy national markets became challenging. Now that the economic recovery is on a relatively sound footing in several key markets, companies with extensive experience in the region should review their business plans in the light of recent developments. For them, this book is intended to serve as a business planning guide as they take a step back from day-to-day operations and engage in a structured process of regional strategy formulation.

PART 1

The Emerging Markets of the Middle East

CHAPTER 2

Middle East Megatrends

The Middle East and North Africa region is going through a period of unprecedented change.[1]

—International Monetary Fund, 2012

Understanding the environment in which a business operates is a critical step in defining business strategy. One effective method for doing this is through environmental scanning, whereby a number of major environmental trends are identified and analyzed. Sometimes these trends are categorized as political, economic, social, technological, legal and environmental (PESTLE). However, such a categorization is not always necessary or helpful, as the most insightful way of looking at what is happening may well be across the boundaries of individual categories. Rather than creating a long list of potentially interesting trends along each of the PESTLE categories, this chapter will only focus on a relatively small number of highly influential developments and will discuss each one in some depth.

The exercise of environmental scanning should usually be done in such a way that the identification and description of the trends are carried out as objectively as possible, based on observable data. In this way, all those with a say in the company's strategy have a common view on the forces that will shape the future and it is only the implications and required courses of action that are open to debate. This is particularly important in the Middle East, where information availability and transparency are not always at desired levels and it requires some careful data gathering and analysis to avoid the pitfalls of proposing strategies based on personal opinions, wishful thinking and hearsay.

This chapter describes the major trends relevant to the Middle Eastern business environment. The relevance of each individual trend will differ greatly by business and country. However, it is certain that each trend discussed will impact business in some important way. Some trends may be familiar to the reader, while others may not be. Even trends that are already known deserve consideration as their implications for business need to be thought through carefully. Companies can add to this analysis by identifying additional developments that are significant to their specific business environment and by thinking through what the various trends described here mean for their regional and national strategies.

Table 2.1. Megatrends Middle East

1. Political instability *and* improving business regulations
2. Energy resources underpin growth
3. The rise of women
4. Turning East
5. Regional integration
6. Value-based consumption
7. Demographics

Trend 1: Political Instability *and* Improving Business Regulations

The Middle East has historically been politically volatile and the last decade has been no exception. The war in Iraq, the ongoing Israeli–Palestinian conflict and tensions over Iran's nuclear program have dominated the news headlines during the first decade of the 21st century. The political upheaval in the Arab world that started in 2010 will also have a fundamental and lasting impact. It is too early to tell what the exact implications of these events will be for business, but an increased level of instability is expected to persist for years in several countries. Events are unfolding at such a rapid pace that any specific coverage of the political changes in the Middle East that started in 2010 would very quickly be out of date and remains out of the scope of this book. In this section, some considerations are offered about the nature of these events and how businesses can manage within these changing contexts.

For a long time, foreign investors believed that most of the regimes in the Middle East provided them with a stable environment to do business.

Ruling families remained in power for decades, thereby providing relatively stable policies and familiar faces for international companies to deal with. For large companies, especially those operating in the natural resources industry, business dealings were made directly between companies and host governments or government-owned companies rather than through highly developed and independent institutions. This way of working made the institutional arrangements in place in a country somewhat less relevant, at least for large investors in the energy industry. However, as countries in the region have started to open up to foreign investors as a part of economic diversification efforts, a more business friendly climate for small- and medium-sized foreign and local investors has emerged in a variety of countries and industries.

Since 2000, Oman, Jordan and Saudi Arabia have entered the WTO, joining Bahrain, Egypt, Kuwait, Qatar and the UAE who have been members since the 1990s. WTO membership forces countries to have a rule-based framework in place for international trade and investment. Saudi Arabia's entry into the WTO in 2005, coupled with the establishment of the Saudi Arabia General Investment Authority (SAGIA), has served as the foundation for a huge increase in FDI in Saudi Arabia.

In parallel, Middle East countries have concluded a number of Free Trade Agreements and Bilateral Investment Treaties with important trading partners, particularly the US. Although the Free Trade Agreement between the GCC and the European Union, which has been under negotiation since 1991, has still not been finalized, several simplifications in tariff structures between the two regions have been realized. Other bilateral trade and investment treaties are continuously being negotiated and implemented, as hopes of a revival of the Doha round of WTO negotiations have subsided.

As countries have started to compete for FDI, restrictions on foreign ownership have been relaxed in many countries and industry sectors, either through legislation that affects a country in its entirety or through the establishment of free trade zones. Countries have started to compete with each other in the quest for FDI and the result has been better business regulation and increased levels of FDI in most countries in the region. This trend is demonstrated by the United Nations' Doing Business report,[2] a publication which measures business regulation in 183 countries, which showed that the Arab countries of the Middle East have continuously increased their average scores along each of the nine dimensions of business regulation. This topic is discussed further in Chapter 4.

Investors need to note that in the case of Middle Eastern countries, in contrast to many Western markets, business-friendly regulations usually mean more regulation rather than less regulation. Countries introduce new laws in order to fill gaps in existing legislation. These new laws are often designed to protect foreign investors and increasingly also protect the environment, workers' rights and consumers. Although these latter stakeholders may not always have the same interests as foreign investors in the short term, in the medium term it is to the benefit of all that they are adequately protected.

Investors need to make their own judgment as to whether new governments in Middle Eastern countries will maintain, accelerate, or reverse these policies toward greater institutional quality and openness to foreign investors in light of the Arab Spring. On the whole, it seems unlikely that a government that is trying to create wealth and job opportunities for its population would make it more difficult or less attractive for foreign investors to establish themselves. Exceptions to this may occur in certain industries where local interests are entrenched and players linked to the state are able to maintain their privileges. However, these situations are more likely to be the exception than the rule. Only if the doom scenario of the rise of extremist governments throughout the Middle East materializes, could it be expected that the business environment would deteriorate significantly.

This leaves the question of what multinational companies can do right now in the face of political uncertainty. In the short term, it is perfectly understandable that some companies have taken a pause in their expansion plans and wait until the dust settles in at least some countries. This is particularly true if there are security risks associated with staff residing in a particular location. Such pauses or slowdowns in expansion provide a good opportunity to reassess the company's plans and be ready for the next phase of growth. However, waiting too long before investing will leave the door open for less risk-averse competitors to gain momentum and benefit from depressed asset prices.

Finally, it is worth noting that perceptions of risk differ greatly depending on one's vantage point. Risk and uncertainty seem greatest when looked at from afar, with television pictures and newspaper stories serving as the main sources of information. Many investors have realized that their perceptions of the Middle East business environment have greatly improved after spending time in the region. Companies that already have a presence in the region are much better able to assess and deal with uncertainty and are more likely to capture opportunities during these volatile times.

In summary, the Middle East is likely to be characterized by continuing political turmoil and improving business regulations in parallel. In order to fully understand the consequences of these conflicting forces, companies benefit greatly from hands-on experience and local knowledge.

Implications

- Companies considering entry into Middle East markets should not wait for some imaginary political *end game* to materialize before taking action. Although putting plans on hold makes sense if volatility becomes extreme, investors waiting for Western-style stability throughout the region will be waiting for a very long time. Successful entrepreneurs in the region operate despite overall political instability. They recognize and manage the specific risks they face in individual markets and retain strategic flexibility as well as a long-term commitment.

- Companies need to think twice before leaving a market when instability strikes. Government officials and business partners never forget who remained loyal to the country during difficult times. Successful reentries into markets are rare. The space left open by departures of businesses is quickly occupied by those who remain committed to a market that is undergoing temporary upheaval. If companies are doubtful about a market in turmoil it is much better to scale-down operations temporarily while maintaining a minimum presence (including the required licenses) in order to be able to scale-up operations again when the business environment improves.

- Political upheaval offers opportunities as well as benefits. For example, the cost of doing business in Bahrain has decreased greatly during the first half of 2011 as residential and commercial rents have fallen. Although some companies have chosen to leave Bahrain, others may find that it still offers an attractive, and now relatively low cost, platform from which the business can serve the region. Another example of business benefiting from upheaval is the hotels and events industry in the UAE during 2011, as tourists and conference organizers have increasingly sought out the relative stability of the UAE.

Trend 2: Energy Resources Underpin Growth

There is no end to the debate on when we will reach *peak oil*, the point in time at which oil production will have reached its maximum level after which a terminal decline is predicted to begin. Some commentators refer to this phenomenon as a myth advanced by oil companies in their efforts to keep prices high. Others predict that a rapid decline in oil reserves is inevitable, driven by demand growth from China and India. The truth is that whatever one's views about the future demand and supply of energy resources are, oil and gas will continue to play a major role in the economies of the region for decades to come. The region controls 45% of the world's proven oil reserves and 26% of global gas reserves. If Iran would be included in the definition of the Middle East, the figures would rise to 55% and 42% for oil and gas respectively. At current production rates, oil reserves are projected to be depleted in 72 years in Saudi Arabia and 94 years in the UAE. In practice, oil and gas reserves in the region have remained stable or have even increased during the last 20 years as new finds have compensated for production. This could mean that energy reserves could last even longer than currently projected.

The real impact of declining oil reserves will be felt much more strongly in the non-OPEC oil exporting countries such as Syria, Oman, Egypt and

Yemen. In these countries, oil production is lower and oil reserves are being depleted more quickly than in OPEC countries. Governments that have relied on oil revenues to maintain financial stability, avoid high levels of taxation and continue subsidies on food and petrol, are now having to make some painful choices. A recent IMF report refers to *eroding buffers* as governments spend their dwindling oil revenues.[3] For these countries, opening up to FDI is not only an effort in economic diversification but also a way to obtain much needed foreign currency reserves and to provide jobs to the increasing number of young people who are entering the labor market.

Table 2.2. *Energy Reserves*

	Oil			Gas		
Country	Reserves (billion barrels)	Share of world total	Reserve/ Production ratio	Gas reserves	Share of world total	Reserve/ Production ratio
Egypt	4.5	0.3%	16.7	2.2	1.2%	36.0
Iraq	115.0	8.3%	>100	3.2	1.7%	>100
Kuwait	101.5	7.3%	>100	1.8	1.0%	>100
Oman	5.5	0.4%	17.4	0.7	0.4%	25.5
Qatar	25.9	1.9%	45.2	25.3	13.5%	>100
Saudi Arabia	264.5	19.1%	72.4	8.0	4.3%	95.5
Syria	2.5	0.2%	17.8	0.3	0.1%	33.2
UAE	97.8	7.1%	94.1	6.0	3.2%	>100
Yemen	2.7	0.2%	27.7	0.5	0.3%	78.3

Source: BP Statistical Review of World Energy 2011.[4]
Reserve-to-production ratio: The remaining amount of reserves, expressed in years, at current production rates.

Implications

- For energy-producing countries, the oil and gas revenues help underpin the government budgets and trade balances. Government budgets of major energy producers such as Saudi Arabia, Kuwait, Qatar and the UAE are consistently in surplus, with oil revenues providing large amounts of investable funds which help to diversify their economies, build infrastructure, provide opportunities for their young and growing populations and ensure there is a social safety net. This will in turn help these countries to maintain political stability. In the UAE, the oil wealth belongs to each individual Emirate and Abu Dhabi has by far the largest share of the UAE's oil reserves. In addition, Abu Dhabi is the largest contributor to the UAE federal budget, resulting in expenditures that benefit all seven emirates of the UAE.

- The oil and gas reserves will provide strong support for a range of industries. These not only include the energy sector, but also energy-intensive industries such as chemicals, aluminum and steel, which are being promoted by energy producers such as Saudi Arabia and Abu Dhabi as vehicles of economic diversification. The combination of energy availability (especially natural gas), cheap labor and low taxes make the region highly attractive for such investments. According to the management consulting firm McKinsey, the Gulf countries have a 30% cost advantage over Europe and China in the production of aluminum, even before taking tax advantages into account.[5] These investments will not only benefit the oil producers but also other countries in the region that open themselves up for investment. As a result of the growth in these energy-intensive industries, several sectors supplying to these industries will also benefit, including logistics, construction and various business services.

Trend 3: The Rise of Women

Despite the continuing presence of significant obstacles, the professional position of women in Arab economies is developing steadily in most countries in the region. The educational achievements and workforce participation levels of Arab women have been increasing continuously.

The rise of women in education can be seen in the number of women attending higher education and by their educational achievements. Women now make up the majority of university student populations in nearly all the Middle Eastern countries for which data is available, including Jordan, Kuwait, Lebanon, the Palestinian Territories, Qatar, Saudi Arabia and the UAE. While at school or university, the educational achievements of women are at a par or better than those of men.[6]

Although women remain vastly underrepresented in the workforce, there has been some improvement in the last decade. Women's participation in the labor market in the MENA region was 22.6% in 2000 and it rose to 24.8% in 2009, while the global average female labor participation rate rose from 52.1% to 52.7% during the same period.[7] In the GCC countries, women are particularly underrepresented in the private sector, where they make up only 1% of the workforce. In most Arab countries, women suffer from higher unemployment rates than men with similar education levels.

Despite these challenges, the new generation of female university graduates now has a number of role models who have reached high-profile positions in business, government and other parts of society. These role models are increasingly celebrated in the media and at universities, thereby inspiring young women to achieve their full potential.[8]

As women graduate from universities and colleges, they increasingly expect to be able to find work that corresponds to their qualifications, abilities and ambitions. The resulting growth in female participation in the labor force provides an additional boost to the working population of the Middle East, on top of the overall population growth. The trends toward higher education levels of women, greater female participation in the workforce and more women in leadership positions are gathering speed, despite the obstacles that remain.

Implications

- Growth in purchasing power of women, as women increasingly control their own expenditures.
- Growth in demand for higher education and professional training, as women stay in education longer.

- Greater pressure on governments to provide professional opportunities to their populations, thereby increasing the pressure behind nationalization programs, particularly in the GCC countries where the expatriate share of the labor force is high.
- Growth in demand for childcare, domestic support and other services to support working families, as Arab women play dual role of parent and working professional.

Trend 4: Turning East

The Middle East has historically played a role as the bridge between Europe and Asia. Today, as the economies of China, India and the rest of Asia power ahead while Europe and the US continue to be caught in a prolonged period of slow growth, the Arab world is increasingly looking East for its business relations. This trend has been well covered in Ben Simpfendorfer's book titled *The New Silk Road: How a Rising Arab World Is Turning Away from the West and Rediscovering China*.[9] Simpfendorfer argues that the revival of business links between the Middle East and the rest of Asia is just a resumption of an ancient pattern of trade between the two regions that has existed for centuries. The recent revival of commercial relations started after the attacks of 9/11 in 2001, when Arab investors felt less welcome in the US and Europe than in the past. Their fear has been realized to a limited extent as some constituencies in the West started to raise objections to Arab Sovereign Wealth Funds and as Congress blocked the acquisition of the US operations of P&O by DP World. However in reality, despite a small number of high-profile issues, Arab investment in the West has not been significantly inhibited.

At the same time, the rapid growth of India, China and other countries in South Asia such as Singapore, Korea, Taiwan, Malaysia and Indonesia have made Asia a more attractive partner for trade and investment. The most straightforward impetus for this trend is the tremendous growth in oil demand from China and India, leading to rapid increases in Middle East oil exports to Asia. In return, the Middle East has increasingly turned eastward for its requirements of manufactured goods and Asia now represents more than half of the region's merchandise imports. China has overtaken the US as the largest exporter to the region. Total trade between the Middle East and the rest of Asia has grown more than fivefold during the first decade of the 21st century.

On the investment front, the two regions are increasingly investing in each other in a diverse range of industry sectors, including petrochemicals, construction, property, transport, energy and infrastructure. Chinese companies are among the major contractors in the construction industry in Saudi Arabia and elsewhere in the region, working on high-profile infrastructure projects such as railways, schools, hospitals and roads. Despite personal lobbying by French President Nicolas Sarkozy, Korean firms are helping the UAE in its developments of nuclear energy and Japanese companies were major contractors for the building of the Dubai metro.

These business links are now underpinned by increased political cooperation, cultural exchanges (including a rapid rise in interest to learn Mandarin) and tourism.[10]

Implications

- Trade and investment between the Middle East and the rest of Asia will continue to grow in importance. Specific industries that are to benefit from this growth include energy, logistics, consumer goods, tourism and travel.
- Western companies established in the Middle East will face increasingly tough competition from Asian players who continue to invest in the region.
- Asian markets will become increasingly attractive for the so-called emerging market multinationals from the Middle East in sectors such as banking, telecommunications, chemicals and hospitality (see Chapter 3).

Trend 5: Regional Integration

It may look highly debatable to place regional integration on a list of major trends in the region. The Gulf Common Currency has been put on hold in 2010 and it does not look like it is going to materialize any

time soon. At the political level, differences between various governments in the region persist and make far reaching political cooperation
an unrealistic prospect, except for the GCC countries. However, other
forces are at work that will serve to continue to promote integration.
These nonpolitical drivers of integration continue to push people and
businesses in the region closer together. The rapidly improving infrastructure in terms of roads, air transport links and telecommunications
serves as a key support mechanism for integration. The planned GCC
rail network will further facilitate the transport of goods and people
across borders.

Recently, the rise of social media and the use of computers, tablets
and mobile phones have further eased communication between people
and businesses across the region. All these developments are supported by
the fact that the Arab countries share Arabic as a common language and
for the most part have English as a second language which also serves as
the common language of the expatriate populations in the region. At the
same time, satellite television has resulted in a largely integrated television and advertising market. A large number of pan-Arab channels with
special themes such as movies, news, sports and cooking now reach a
regional audience.

An additional impetus to integration is provided by significant migra-
tion flows, especially from the Levant to the GCC countries. Although
it would be incorrect to call the GCC countries melting pots of Arabic
cultures, these migrant professionals do facilitate and promote a greater
level of integration between Arab countries.

These forces have also supported the rise of regional multinational
companies in various sectors, including banking, telecommunications,
construction, property, transport and education (see Chapter 3). Successful companies in national markets have typically first considered foreign
markets within the region for their international expansion. Companies
from outside the region also tend to have regional strategies, coordinating
national operations from a single regional hub office while marketing a
similar product or service in a number of countries. The internationalization of the strategies and operations of companies is thereby acting as
another force for regional integration.

Only at the political level has change been slow. Several years ago, the Gulf Monetary Union was planned to be in place by 2010. The global economic crisis, the euro crisis and regional political factors have led to the plan being shelved for the time being. In any case, the existing dollar peg or currency basket peg of many countries in the region is stable and the values of the GCC currencies hardly fluctuate against each other. Any form of monetary union would therefore not have a significant impact on foreign investors, unless it would be accompanied by other monetary, economic or institutional changes. The most significant moves toward political cooperation have also been taking place within the GCC. Accession talks with Morocco and Jordan started in 2011 and discussions on further political integration have been gathering pace during 2012.

With respect to other elements of political and economic integration, there is an increasing realization that it is highly inefficient to negotiate free trade agreements on a strictly bilateral basis. These days, economic agreements are more likely to be negotiated at the regional level (either Arab countries or just the GCC), enabling countries to combine their strengths and make effective use of the resources that are required for negotiations. This is even more relevant now that the WTO's Doha round has come to a halt and countries are taking step-by-step approaches to liberalize trade instead of working toward an all-encompassing global agreement.

In summary, the trend toward greater integration is continuing at a steady pace at the level of the citizen, the economy and the region's physical infrastructure.

Implications

- Although major variations remain between countries in the region and market segments within each country, pan Arab marketing and promotion strategies are becoming possible, especially for consumer goods companies.
- Intraregional transport, trade and investment volumes will continue to grow. Although historically Arab countries have traded more with other regions than with each other, this pattern is changing.

Trend 6: Value-Based Consumption

The Middle East consumers are increasingly purchasing goods and services that are in line with their values and beliefs. This trend is best illustrated by the growth in Islamic banking, which continues to expand throughout the region and beyond. In 2011, Ernst & Young reported that Islamic banking assets in the MENA region have doubled during the period 2005–2010 to $416 billion and are expected to double again during the next 5 years.[11] Islamic banking assets now represent 14% of the banking market in the MENA region overall and 26% in the GCC countries.

The trend toward value-based consumption is broader than Islamic finance alone. Traditional media and the new social media are increasingly effective in spreading information about corporate behavior regarding such issues as the environment, Middle East politics and other topics of concern to consumers. Although starting form a low base, environmental awareness is growing quickly. The opportunity to catch up to the standards of other countries will result in rapid growth of environmentally sustainable industries, such as waste recycling and alternative energy. This trend is supported by several other developments on the supply side of the equation, particularly the scarcity of water and enduring electricity supply problems, even in countries with ample energy reserves. These supply-side issues are encouraging governments to be more favorable to sustainable production and consumption.

Implications

- The markets for Islamic finance and insurance will continue to grow strongly. Various countries from the Middle East and Asia will compete to become knowledge centers for the emerging field of Islamic finance. Banks from the Middle East will prioritize countries with large Muslim populations such as Malaysia and Indonesia for their international expansion.
- Government actions to change the incentives away from polluting products will lead to growth of some product areas

at the expense of others. The demand for natural gas is set to increase as a cleaner and cheaper way to generate electricity. The price for water, electricity, petrol and waste collection will progressively reflect more of the true cost associated with them. Projects in the fields of solar and nuclear energy will become more prevalent.

- As energy and water become more expensive, buildings will be designed with energy and water consumption in mind (so-called *green buildings*). Environmentally friendly products such as organic food and biodegradable bags will face large increases in demand. However, an end to the ubiquitous 4×4 cars on Middle Eastern roads is not to be expected anytime soon.

Trend 7: Demographics

Much of the Middle East growth story is about demographics. Although the overall trends are well known, it is worth investigating beneath the overall statement of *population growth* and see where and how it will have an impact on business.

The Middle East boasts a young population which is predicted to grow by 81% from 217 million in 2010 to 392 million in 2050. By 2050, the Middle East's population is projected to be larger than that of the European Union's six largest countries combined (that is all of Germany, France, Italy, United Kingdom, Spain and Poland taken together). If neighboring countries Turkey and Iran were to be included in the definition of the Middle East, then its population would approach 600 million people by 2050. Except for Africa, no other region in the world is projected to grow so rapidly.

Underneath this overall trend there are several significant developments to watch. Given the existing age profile of the population, the most rapid population growth will be in the working age segment; young people currently at school and university will enter the working population in unprecedented numbers. This development provides both opportunities and threats. The growing population of working age should make it possible to support the equally expanding population of elderly people without too much difficulty, unlike in Europe and Japan where the aging of the population poses huge financial and social challenges. At the same time, these young people entering the labor market will demand meaningful jobs and sufficient income to be able to start a family of their own. The number of people entering the labor market is much higher than the jobs that can be offered by national governments and state-controlled enterprises. Consequently, the growth of the private sector and individual entrepreneurship are increasingly essential in maintaining both economic growth and social stability.

In parallel with the overall population growth, there are two other relevant demographic trends:

- Despite continuing population growth, fertility rates are on the decline, as young people start their families later in life and women have fewer children. This trend is in turn supported by the increasing number of women who obtain higher education and enter the workforce (see Trend 3). However, both fertility rates and family size remain higher than those in Western countries.
- The size of major cities will continue to grow rapidly, especially in countries with large populations and relatively low urbanization rates, such as Egypt, Syria and Yemen. This urbanization will place an increasing demand on the infrastructure in major cities, including roads, electricity supply, schools and hospitals.

Implications

- Growing markets in many product and service sectors, including food, water, electricity, housing, health care, financial services and transport.
- Growing pressure to reduce dependency on foreign labor (especially skilled labor) in order to provide greater opportunities for local citizens. This pressure will be strongest in countries that currently rely heavily on foreign workers such as Kuwait, Saudi Arabia, Qatar and the UAE.

Table 2.3. Demographic Data

Country	Population (in millions)			2050 population as multiple of 2010	Percent of population by age		Percent of population urban
	(2010)	(2025)	(2050)		Under 15 years	Over 65 years	
Bahrain	1.3	1.6	2.0	1.6	20	2	100
Egypt	80.4	103.6	137.7	1.7	33	4	43
Iraq	31.5	44.7	64.0	2.0	41	3	67
Jordan	6.5	8.5	11.8	1.8	37	3	83
Kuwait	3.1	4.1	5.4	1.7	23	2	98
Lebanon	4.3	4.7	5.0	1.2	25	10	87
Oman	3.1	4.2	7.5	1.8	29	2	72
Palestinian Territory	4.0	6.0	9.4	2.3	44	3	83
Qatar	1.7	2.1	2.6	1.5	15	1	100
Saudi Arabia	29.2	35.7	49.8	1.7	38	2	81
Syria	22.5	28.6	36.9	1.6	36	3	54
UAE	5.4	7.0	9.4	1.8	19	1	83
Yemen	23.6	34.5	52.2	2.2	45	3	29

Source: Population Reference Bureau.[12]

Governments are using a *carrot and stick* approach to the nationalization of the labor force. The supply of qualified nationals is promoted through improved education and various national employment agencies, while regulations on quotas of national employees are beginning to be expanded, monitored and increasingly enforced.

- There is a great need for education and training to prepare the young population for work in the private sector. There will be increasing support for local entrepreneurship initiatives, encouraging young people to create their own jobs.

- Increasing pressure on scarce natural resources, particularly water which is set to become the *next oil* in terms of strategic importance as a resource.

- Increasing pressure on food prices and food supply. Most GCC countries find it difficult to grow enough food for their expanding populations. The vast amounts of water consumed by agriculture in these desert climates will make it increasingly expensive to do so. Middle Eastern countries have been looking abroad for food supplies as well as for mechanisms to obtain food security through land purchases, sometimes raising political concerns in the process. Such developments provide export opportunities for countries and companies in other part of the region (e.g., Lebanon, Syria), provided they can supply the products required by GCC markets at consistent quality levels.

Conclusion

Each one of these trends will naturally affect various countries and industries in different ways, but all the developments discussed here apply to all countries in the region at least to some extent. The trends can serve as a basis for environmental scanning for companies' own strategic plans for the region. First, for each trend, an assessment can be made with respect to opportunities and threats that arise from it. At a macro level, the trends point toward significant growth in many markets, including housing, education, health, consumer goods, telecommunications, financial services, leisure and travel. A deeper analysis of the trends discussed in this chapter and potentially other trends will help companies determine which geographies and customer segments will show the most rapid growth. The fact that a market will grow does not necessarily make it attractive for a company; this also depends on factors such as regulations, competitive intensity, institutions and the unique capabilities that an investor brings to the market. Still, the key developments discussed here can be a good starting point from which companies work out the implications for their strategies and identify other trends that may be specifically relevant to them.

Some of the developments described may also represent challenges, rather than just opportunities. In this case, companies need to devise strategies for dealing with the challenges presented. This is particularly the case for political risk and institutional quality, topics that are discussed further in Chapter 4.

CHAPTER 3

The Rise of Multinational Companies from the Middle East

Emerging multinationals you've never heard of could eat your lunch,
take your job, or possibly be your next business partner or employer.
—Antoine van Agtmael[1]

A development that warrants special consideration by investors is that of multinational companies originating from the Middle East. The topic of emerging market multinationals is seen as a frontier topic in the field of International Business research. Multinational companies from emerging markets are regarded as fierce competitors in their home markets and increasingly in developed markets as well. Today, nearly all the research and business writing on emerging market multinationals bypasses the increasingly international and successful companies from the Middle East. Antoine van Agtmael's book *The Emerging Markets Century* contains a listing of 25 *world-class emerging multinationals*, of which not a single one originates from the Middle East. More recent books on *Emerging Multinationals in Emerging Markets*[2] and *MNEs from Emerging Markets*[3] profile successful multinationals from over 15 countries, with not a single mention of a company from the Arab Middle East.

The reason for this lack of attention to the Middle East is not that there are no successful multinational companies around, as will be demonstrated in this chapter. A possible explanation may be that successful multinationals from the Middle East are a recent phenomenon, are still small in number, are largely absent from branded consumer goods industries and often have a regional rather than a global focus. Most of the companies featured in this chapter have only risen to prominence during the past decade and several maintain a regional rather than a global focus. Although many of the companies listed are celebrated within their own countries and even regionally, they still lack the global name recognition of their peers from other emerging markets.

In terms of size, Arab multinationals remain relatively small. SABIC is the only Arab company that is part of the Fortune 500 (ranked 210).[4] The region is better represented on the Forbes Global 2000[5] ranking of the world's largest stock market–quoted companies ranked by market capitalization, with a total of 53 companies on the list. The companies on this list come from throughout the region, with Bahrain, Egypt, Jordan, Kuwait, Lebanon, Oman, Qatar, Saudi Arabia and the UAE all having at least one company represented. However, because over half of the companies on this list are active in the banking sector, often with only a national or at best a regional geographic focus, it cannot be said that these companies are all true emerging market multinationals.

A more forward-looking view is provided by the 2011 report of the Boston Consulting Group (BCG) on *Global Challengers*,[6] which includes companies that are *already sizeable, are globally expansive and are taking a run at traditional multinational companies*. Out of the 100 Global Challengers identified by BCG, five companies come from the Middle East (El Sewedy Electric from Egypt, SABIC from Saudi Arabia and DP World, Emirates Airline and Etisalat from the UAE). According to the BCG report, during the period 2000–2009 these firms have grown their sales three times as fast as the nonfinancial companies of the S&P 500, without sacrificing margins. Other companies that are expanding aggressively in international markets include the major telecom operators (including Qatar Telecom, Etisalat, Saudi Telecom), property and construction firms such as Emaar, Arabtec and Depa, as well as some of the major banks that are expanding rapidly in Asia.

Some analysts argue that the success of multinational companies from the Middle East is due to strong links with government, protected home markets and access to cheap finance, resulting in unfair competition in international markets. Although it is true that some companies in the region benefit from strong ties to the authorities, the same may be said of Chinese companies or even of certain Western multinationals. In any case, focusing on only the government links takes the attention away from some of the more profound reasons for success that can serve as inspiration to those looking to collaborate or to compete with these emerging players both in the Middle East and at home.

Who Are the Emerging Multinationals of the Middle East?

A listing of leading multinational companies from the region is by definition a subjective exercise. In order to provide some guidance, the common characteristics of *emerging world-class multinationals* as defined by Antoine van Agtmael may be considered. According to van Agtmael, world class multinationals:

- Are widely considered as leaders in their industry on a global, not just a national or regional basis.
- Have a truly global presence in exports, and, often, production.
- Have a top-three market share in enough countries to be a global player.
- Are globally competitive not just in price but also in quality, technology, design and management.
- Can be benchmarked against the biggest and best in the world.[7]

Based on these criteria, the companies listed in Table 3.1 can be considered to be either emerging world-class multinationals or on their way to getting there. SABIC is the world's sixth largest chemical company. Emirates is the world's largest airline measured by scheduled international passenger kilometers. DP World is among the world's top three port companies, operating 60 marine terminals across six continents. The vision of Aramex is to be among the world's top five logistics and transportation companies. Other companies on the list are equally impressive in terms of past achievements, current position and future potential.

The companies are active in a range of sectors and come from various countries, although the UAE takes account of a disproportionate share. Many Arab multinationals have started to internationalize first of all within their own region and most companies on the list still generate a large share of their sales from the Middle East. However, each company has made at least some significant steps in other parts of the world and some companies have now developed into truly global players.

Table 3.1. Leading Middle East Multinationals

Company	Industry	Home country	Revenues (2011) (US$ billions)
Agility	Logistics	Kuwait	4.8
Aramex	Logistics	Jordan	0.7
DP World	Ports	UAE	3.0
Emirates	Air transport	UAE	15.6
Etihad	Air transport	UAE	4.1
Jumeirah	Hotels	UAE	n/a
Orascom	Telecom	Egypt	3.9
Qatar Airways	Air transport	Qatar	n/a
SABIC	Chemicals and plastics	Saudi Arabia	50.6

Most of the companies on the list have their national government as a key shareholder. Government ownership has provided stability and access to finance during the early years of the life of these companies but can no longer really be considered as the major reason of their international success today. As these companies have expanded globally, their shareholder structure gives them little advantage in global markets. This point will be further elaborated below.

Strategies for Success

The question remains as to how these companies are achieving their success. Although little in-depth research has been carried out on this topic until now, there are a few common themes that can be applied to most players.

No Legacy

In several industries, Middle Eastern companies have been able to achieve global success due to the absence of outdated technology, equipment and work processes. Especially the oil-rich countries of the GCC have benefited from starting their commercial development from a low base with plenty of capital available due to booming oil revenues. This starting position has enabled airlines such as Emirates, Qatar Airways and Etihad Airways to operate without labor contracts that oblige it to pay senior pilots above market rates. It allows them to operate from relatively new airports with young and efficient fleets and employ the latest technology without being concerned about an installed base of legacy equipment.

Similarly, the region's banks have not had to worry about oversized branch networks that have become less useful as ATMs and internet banking take away the need for branches to process transactions. While banks in Europe and the US are trimming down their branch networks due to cost pressures and the introduction of new technology, many Middle Eastern banks are still opening branches as a result of increases in customer numbers. As new branches are opened, they are able to ensure that all of them are fitted out with the latest technology.

These are just two examples of industries in which Middle East competitors can immediately jump to international best practices and innovate by pioneering new business models. Players in other industries in the Middle East have benefited in similar ways from an ability to start from scratch, including hotels, airports, retailers, manufacturers and telecom operators.

Location Advantages

Like all companies, Middle East competitors try to make the most of their location advantages. The region's location advantages arise essentially from the fact that it sits at the crossroads between Europe, Asia and Africa and the presence of energy resources.

The Middle East is strategically located between the exporters of manufactured goods from East Asia and the markets of Europe. This has helped DP World to develop the Dubai port into a major trans-shipment center and the airports of Dubai, Abu Dhabi and Doha to become global transit terminals. One-third of the world's population lives within a 5-hour flight radius of these airports. This geographic positioning has also helped the travel and tourism industry generally, with increasing visitors from Russia, China, India and elsewhere who come to the region for leisure and business. It seems that whenever one source of tourist arrivals suffers, another country stands ready to make up the difference.

The region's location at the intersection of three continents has also driven the international expansion of Middle East multinationals. Companies active in a range of industries including property development, telecommunications, leisure and banking have chosen to expand into the rapidly growing markets in Asia and Africa rather than the more mature and saturated markets in Europe. Both local and foreign companies are increasingly locating their regional headquarters in the Middle East, with definitions of the region ranging from Africa and the Middle East to MENA and MENASA (Middle East North Africa South Asia).

The second major location advantage of the region is based on energy resources. This advantage goes much further than just the wealth that is generated from exploiting the region's oil and gas resources. For example, the petrochemical industry in Saudi Arabia has benefited from its proximity to oil supplies and to the presence of natural gas which was previously flared as it was freed up during oil production. This has allowed petrochemical companies to purchase gas at much reduced rates compared with global gas prices. As international competitors are accusing Saudi Arabian chemical companies of price dumping and as gas demand increases, there is pressure to increase domestic gas prices. Still, the proximity to energy resources has benefited intensive industries such as chemicals, fertilizers and aluminum.

Operational Excellence

Several factors have helped Middle Eastern companies to become highly efficient operators. The absence of a legacy infrastructure and processes has been a key factor, as described above. The availability of relatively cheap land and labor has also helped to keep a lid on costs over time. Even though cities and industrial areas have grown, there has generally been enough space available to expand. As many countries have accepted a large influx of foreign labor, wage costs have remained low, especially for unskilled and semi-skilled labor.

These factors, together with the use of expatriate and local expertise, have resulted in some of the leading companies being highly effective operators. There is generally a strong emphasis on managing repetitive work processes in highly standardized ways. Although this may some-times lead to a loss of flexibility, it does result in standard processes working well, resulting in high quality levels and low costs at the leading companies. The next challenge for Middle East multinationals will be to build on their operational excellence and lead the way in breakthrough innovations.

Aramex is a prime example of a company that thrives on operational excellence. Aramex started as a local logistics company in Jordan in 1982. Now it is a genuine international operator with operations in 58 countries that continues to expand. In 2011 alone it made significant investments in South Africa, Kenya, Ireland and China. Aramex has been able to achieve this impressive growth by delivering excellence in transport, logistics and supply chain services in rapidly growing markets. Starting without a legacy infrastructure it has chosen an *asset-light* model (through franchising arrangements), avoiding to tie up its capital in heavy assets and thereby enabling a focus on customer ser-vice, information technology and innovation. This model has allowed it to fully benefit from the growth in its original markets, capture market share and ensure that funding is available for investment in new markets. In 1997, Aramex became the first Arab company to be listed on the NASDAQ exchange. Since then it has been taken private and subsequently refloated a part of its shares on the Dubai Financial Market in 2005.

Government Support

Many successful emerging market multinationals have strong links to their home country government. These links can be in the form of ownership links, provision of finance as well as in customer–supplier relationships. Some Western competitors complain that emerging market multinationals benefit from protected markets and cheap access to finance at home which helps to generate cash, which can then be used to obtain an unfair advantage in international markets. Besides the occasional investment in European football teams, there is in fact little evidence to support this view. Arab governments are on the whole rational economic actors and want their international investments to generate proper financial returns. As companies operate across the world, they will pay taxes in whichever country they do business in and will need to comply with local rules and regulations. In this sense, multinationals from the MNE play by the same rules as any other company.

One area in which government support has played a role is in what can best be labeled as a systems approach to economic development. A systems approach refers to the idea that private and public sector development should go hand in hand in order to develop hard and soft infrastructure that is conducive to the development of world-class companies. Until now, Dubai has been the most successful entity implementing such systems thinking. Consider, for example, the travel and hospitality sector in Dubai which consists of airlines, the airport, hotels, retailers and various other players. As the airport expands, Emirates Airlines can operate more flights and Dubai Duty Free (already the world's largest airport retailer) continues to grow. Meanwhile, local hotels and retailers receive more visitors and expand. All this makes Dubai a more attractive venue for exhibitions and conferences, which in turn leads to increased visitor numbers. This sophisticated travel and tourism infrastructure is now supported by educational ventures such as Jumeirah's Academy of Hospitality Management and the Emirates Aviation College. In this way, each component of the chain stands to gain from the growth and success of the others and a self-reinforcing virtuous circle arises.

Although it is entirely justified to debate what types of government support are useful or appropriate in order to build such an ecosystem, there is no denying that the success of these different players is at least to some extent due to a deliberate government strategy. The successful companies in the Middle East are by no means the only ones to benefit from this approach, as evidenced by similarly successful players from Singapore, China and elsewhere.

Emirates Airlines: Bringing It All Together

The multiple benefits of a lack of legacy, location advantages, operational excellence and government-led systems thinking are most clearly demonstrated by the continuing rise of Emirates Airlines. Founded in 1985, Emirates is now among the world's top 10 airlines, ranks first in terms of scheduled international passenger miles flown and has the world's largest fleet of Airbus A380 planes. Based on 2010 profits, Emirates is the world's most profitable airline. Profits have declined during 2011, mainly as a result of fuel price increases and exchange rate movements, but passenger growth continues to be high and profitability remains sound.

Emirates makes the most of its location advantage, with many passengers using Dubai just as a stopover point. The airline's home base is ideally located between Australasia, Europe and Africa and even serves as a hub for American passengers.

The company is only just over 25 years old and benefits from one of the youngest fleets in the industry. As Airbus launched its fuel-efficient A380 super jets, Emirates quickly became the largest customer, allowing the company to fly long-distance routes into congested airports with great efficiency. The company's lack of legacy has also helped to design customer service standards from scratch and manage them tightly. Labor costs have been kept down as staff are recruited globally. All this has meant that Emirates is a highly efficient operator that has been consistently profitable.

The company has also benefited from the Dubai aviation ecosystem. Dubai International Airport has grown in line with passenger traffic and a new concourse dedicated to the Emirates A380 fleet is to be opened. The development of the airline and that of Dubai's tourism and business sectors continue to benefit each other greatly. As one grows, the others benefit.

Perhaps as a consequence of its success, Emirates gets criticized frequently and strongly by its competitors. The airline has been accused of benefiting from subsidized fuel, zero taxes and preferential access at Dubai airport. Even European governments have been said to subsidize the airline through export credit guarantee schemes that serve to promote exports by European manufacturers such as Airbus. Emirates continues to counter each of these arguments one by one. Without dealing with each charge of unfair competition specifically here, the following two quotes from the Economist and UBS are instructive.

> The charges of unfair competition from the likes of Lufthansa, Air France-KLM and Air Canada fail to stack up. Although it is government-owned, Emirates has been profitable in every year but one since it started. Its fast growing fleet ... is financed conventionally. It pays the same price for fuel as other airlines and the same fees at its home airport.
>
> —*The Economist*, June 3, 2010[10]

UBS analyzed the accounts of the company and came to the following conclusion:

> An overview of the audited financial accounts contains no material surprises once one gets used to seeing consistent profits at an airline ... Emirates' key competitive advantage is its relative youth (the fleet and the company), the location and efficiency of the Dubai hub and strong management.[11]
>
> —UBS report, quoted in *Subsidy. Myths and Facts about Emirates and Our Industry,* Emirates.

Emirates Airlines is here to stay as a formidable competitor to airlines across the globe and several other Middle East airlines are equally dynamic. Etihad Airways and Qatar Airways are following a similar hub model as Emirates. In the low-cost segment, Air Arabia is a true multinational operator with hubs in Sharjah (UAE), Egypt and Morocco, with each hub location having its own geographic focus in terms of flight destinations.

Conclusion

Understanding emerging multinational companies form the Middle East is important for potential investors for multiple reasons. As demonstrated here, a number of companies from the Middle East are emerging as international competitors. Their initial focus on the Middle East, Africa and

Asia may make these companies go unnoticed by European and American companies initially, but this does not diminish their relevance in a global market where most of the economic growth is coming from emerging markets. These companies are not only competitors but may also serve as partners, either by helping foreign companies to enter the Middle East or as new entrants in Western markets.

By understanding the sources of competitive advantage of these companies, foreign investors can try to supplement their own strengths with sources of advantage available to companies from the Middle East.

CHAPTER 4

Institutions and Risk

Reforms will need to provide more equal access to economic opportunities, promote transparency, improve access to credit by strengthening financial market infrastructures, and, more generally, enhance the business environment by cutting red tape and streamlining rules and procedures.

—International Monetary Fund, Regional Economic Outlook, Middle East and Central Asia, April 2012.[1]

Institutional voids are obstacles for doing business in emerging markets but they can also be a source of advantage for those companies— foreign or domestic—that have local knowledge, privileged access to resources, or other capabilities that can help substitute for missing market institutions.

—Tarun Khanna and Krishna G. Palepu *Winning in Emerging Markets, a Road Map for Strategy and Execution.*[2]

International investors are greatly impacted by institutional factors and the risks associated with the political and business environment in a country. When referring to institutions, investors are typically concerned about the formal and informal governance structures in an economy and the effectiveness with which the rules are enforced. Sometimes the term is defined more broadly as the level of development of any market intermediary, not just regulators, that helps to facilitate transactions between buyers and sellers. When taking this perspective, countries with undeveloped institutions may make it difficult for companies to do business, but these countries also offer opportunities for businesses to step in and play intermediary roles that are currently not adequately fulfilled.

Risks related to a country's political and business environment can take many forms. Political risk has been defined by Franklin Root as "the uncertainty over the continuation of present political conditions and government policies in the foreign host country that are critical to the profitability of an actual or proposed equity/contractual business arrangement."[3] Root identifies four types of risks faced by international investors: general instability, expropriation risk, operations risk and transfer risk. General instability may affect the business environment negatively in various ways, as demonstrated during 2011 by the events in Egypt and elsewhere in the region. Although foreign investors have not been *forced* to abandon their projects in Egypt, the economy has taken a direct hit from which it will take some time to recover. As a result, many investors have halted or delayed their investment projects in the country and FDI has plummeted.

A second type of risk relates to expropriation risk, which can be of concern particularly in the energy and banking sectors. In practice, expropriation is an extremely rare event in the Arab Middle East. Although it cannot be ignored, particularly in the light of regime changes in the region, the probability of significant expropriations remains very low. There has been a plethora of Bilateral Investment Treaties (BITs) in recent years between countries in the region and elsewhere. The main purpose of BITs is for countries to specify in advance the rules that would apply in case of an expropriation event, dealing with issues such as the process to follow and the compensation to be paid. The BITs give additional comfort to investors that they will be treated according to agreed rules in the unlikely event of an expropriation of their assets.

Thirdly, operations risk refers to any changes in government policies that may affect any aspect of company's operations, including marketing, finance, human resources, or any other function. Operations risk is clearly higher in countries where government instability is high. However, there is also a positive side to operations risk; government policies may change in ways that are either detrimental or beneficial for foreign investors. As policies change, incumbent multinational companies are often best placed to benefit from the changed environment, provided they are not locked in to contractual arrangements that make it expensive for them to change their ways of operating. In this way, entry into a market is not only valuable by itself but also provides a *real option* of expanding or reducing the company's investment when circumstances change.

As with financial options, the greater the volatility, the more valuable is the option. In this way, the real option value of being in a country can be highest in volatile circumstances.

The fourth type of risk identified by Root is transfer risk, which refers to the risk of companies not being able to repatriate their profits to their home country. Although both expropriation risk and transfer risk events are extremely rare in the Middle East, they are worthy of consideration. The more common areas of investor concern are general stability and operations risk in terms of changes to regulations or a deterioration in general business environment that may affect international investors. An individual analysis of the types of regulations that impact a company and the risk of such regulations changing is required for every investment that a company considers.

Risk Analysis

Managers usually perceive the Middle East to be associated with high risk and poor institutional development. These perceptions make an accurate assessment of the countries' institutions and stability highly relevant. On the one hand, companies need to enter markets with full knowledge of the institutional environment and the associated risks. On the other hand, avoiding markets because of perceived risks may lead companies to miss out on important growth opportunities. Navigating a path along these different considerations requires information, analysis and decision-making.

The remainder of this chapter includes an overview of three of the most in-depth measures of institutional quality in the Arab Middle East and gives guidance on how to utilize the data. Although the available measures provide a wealth of useful information, great care must be taken with their use and interpretation. An overall measure of a country's business environment or risk profile should not be used naively in justifying investment decisions. Instead, companies should make a profile of which aspects of the business and regulatory environment has the greatest potential impact on their particular investment and then use the various reports as a starting point to gathering the relevant information. It also needs to be kept in mind that markets that are considered as *difficult* can provide the best opportunities, especially because competitive intensity may well be less severe in markets that are avoided by some of the global players.

The Regulatory Environment

The World Bank's Doing Business report provides a much quoted source of information on the ease of doing business in 183 countries around the world.[4] The report publishes measures and rankings on regulatory aspects of doing business along nine steps in the life cycle of a company, ranging from starting a business to closing a business. Both strictly legal aspects and *time and motion* indicators (i.e., how long a procedure takes in practice) are captured in the report.

The Doing Business report stresses the point that, contrary to perceived wisdom in many Western countries, businesses in emerging markets are not always looking for less regulation. New regulations that strengthen the effectiveness of markets and institutions in a country are typically welcomed by investors. In the Middle East, countries are working on issues that are not always adequately covered by existing legislation, such as consumer protection, investor protection, intellectual property rights, corporate governance and bankruptcy legislation. In these areas, new legislation clarifies the rules of the road and provides comfort to investors. The World Bank describes the underlying philosophy as follows:

> "A fundamental premise of *Doing Business* is that economic activity requires good rules—rules that establish and clarify property rights and reduce the cost of resolving disputes; rules that increase the predictability of economic interactions and provide contractual partners with certainty and protection against abuse. The objective is regulations designed to be efficient, accessible to all and simple in their implementation. *Doing Business* gives higher scores in some areas for stronger property rights and investor protections, such as stricter disclosure requirements in related-party transactions. Through indicators benchmarking 183 economies, *Doing Business* sheds light on how easy or difficult it is for a local entrepreneur to open and run a small to medium-size business while complying with relevant regulations."[5]

Despite the fact that the rankings are often quoted among international investors and policymakers, it needs to be kept in mind that the indicators refer to the ease of business for *domestic* entrepreneurs in *small- and medium-sized businesses*. International investors may be particularly interested in some specific components of a country's regulatory environment, such as enforcing contracts, but they may care less about regulations with respect to getting credit or registering property for local residents. An additional area of concern about the report is that it has received so much attention globally that now some policymakers seem to have been tempted to introduce reforms primarily as a means of improving a country's ranking in the table. Such behavior is actually encouraged by the World Bank which has added a Doing Business Reform Simulator on its website, allowing policymakers to see how a certain regulatory change can impact a country's ranking. In 2010, the Economist commented on the Doing Business report:

> "The remarkable leaps that a few countries have made in the league table have led to suspicions that some governments are gaming the system by paper reforms to bump up their score without making much difference to the ease of doing business in the country."[6]

As with all ratings and rankings, investors are encouraged to look below the surface. Besides getting an overall picture of which country is *business friendly*, investors should use the report to understand those specific aspects of the business environment that matter most to them. The report deals with nine aspects of doing business, each of which is in turn subdivided into three or four detailed indicators.

Table 4.1 shows the overall ranking of Arab countries as well as the position along three dimensions of particular importance to foreign investors: trading across borders, protecting investors and enforcing contracts.

Several important observations can be made from the table. First, there is a tremendous variation between the countries in both the overall rankings and the scores on specific indicators. The overall ranking scores vary from 12th for Saudi Arabia to 164th for Iraq. This result demonstrates again that the Middle East cannot be treated as a single region, but that each country has important individual characteristics.

Table 4.1. Doing Business Indicators, 2012. Rankings Out of
183 Countries

	Overall ranking	Trading across borders	Protecting investors	Enforcing contracts
Bahrain	38	49	79	114
Egypt	110	64	79	147
Iraq	164	180	122	140
Jordan	96	58	122	130
Kuwait	67	112	29	117
Lebanon	104	93	97	120
Oman	49	47	97	107
Palestinian Territory	131	114	46	93
Qatar	36	57	97	95
Saudi Arabia	12	18	17	138
Syria	134	122	111	175
UAE	33	5	122	134
Yemen	99	118	133	38

Source: Doing Business in a more transparent world, World Bank, 2012.[7]

Second, it is remarkable that in terms of the overall ease of doing business, the top six countries in the list are all GCC member states. The
GCC countries have been working steadily to improve their business
environment as part of efforts to diversify their economies away from
natural resources. Third, the Middle East countries typically score less
well on measures of investor protection and contract enforcement than
on the other dimensions of Doing Business, such as measures related to
trading across borders. The issue of contract enforcement in particular
is an important consideration for international investors and warrants
attention when making location decisions in the region. Still, it would
be wrong to conclude that contracts are not enforced in the Middle East.
The data reported on contract enforcement are based on individual measures for the time, cost and procedural complexity of resolving a commercial lawsuit between two domestic businesses. Although it is true that
the time and costs associated with resolving disputes through the courts
are generally high, this does not mean that contracts are not enforce-
able. Arab governments are introducing reforms to speed up the judicial

process, for example, through the establishment of specialized courts and greater use of information technology. International investors can also take the issue of contract enforcement into account when choosing where within a country to set up. For example, the Dubai International Financial Centre (DIFC) has its own English language courts based largely on UK commercial legislation and is regulated by an independent body, the Dubai Financial Services Authority (DFSA). Many companies have set up in the DIFC partly in order to benefit from this regulatory framework. In November 2011, the DIFC courts have made their jurisdiction available to Dubai-based companies operating outside the DIFC.

DIFC Courts

Businesses in Dubai can now opt to take their disputes to the Dubai International Financial Centre (DIFC) courts, following an overhaul of the Gulf emirate's commercial legal system.

The Dubai government on Monday widened the court's jurisdiction to allow companies based outside the tax-free business park to bring their cases before the common law court.

Under the new rules, companies can opt to resolve their disputes in DIFC courts if both parties agree to the court's jurisdiction. Contracts can also include a clause binding both parties to use the English-language court in the event of a disagreement.

"[The decision] provides businesses with more choice; choice to have their cases heard in Arabic or English, using civil or common law procedures," Michael Hwang, Chief Justice of the DIFC courts, told Arabian Business.

Companies outside the free zone were previously tied to bringing cases before the Arabic-language Dubai courts in the event of a dispute.

"This move will further reinforce Dubai's reputation as the business hub of the region, and attract business to invest in Dubai that may otherwise have established elsewhere."

Cases can be brought before the Court of First Instance, the Small Claims Tribunal, and the Court of Appeal.

Source: Arabian Business, November 1, 2011.[8]

In general, international investors should take the necessary steps to avoid litigation with partners and suppliers. It must be realized that resorting to the courts for the resolution of commercial disputes is much more of a last resort option in the Middle East than in, for example, the US, where litigation is more common.

In addition to its global report, the World Bank also publishes a report that is specific to the Arab world. In its most recent Doing Business in the Arab World[9] report, it is reported that Arab countries made significant progress in the last few years along several dimensions of the business environment, including the ease of starting a business, the establishment of the legal infrastructure for credit information bureaus and the upgrading of customs facilities in ports in several countries. As a result, the average score of the Arab countries for each of the dimensions of Doing Business has steadily improved since 2006. The report highlights inadequate bankruptcy proceedings as a major obstacle to entrepreneurs and stresses the need to decriminalize bankruptcy and quicker judicial procedures to allow for an orderly and rapid reallocation of assets. The issue of bankruptcy proceedings has come to light during the economic crisis of 2008, when for the first time a significant number of companies entered into payment difficulties. The 2009 *Survey on Insolvency Systems in the Middle East and North Africa*,[10] published by the Hawkamah Institute for Corporate Governance and the World Bank came to the following conclusions:

- Insolvency systems in MENA are generally inconsistent with international best practice.
- The Gulf States have stronger insolvency laws than other MENA countries, but need to improve credit information systems and dealing with cross-border issues.
- Both Gulf and non-Gulf States have room for improvement compared with international standards and practice, particularly in the area of reorganization of companies.
- Based on Common Law and the advantage of *purpose-built*, the DIFC insolvency framework is the most robust and highest rated in the region.
- Strengthening and modernizing insolvency laws are crucial to mitigating the risks and effects of economic and financial crises on MENA countries.

In summary, the Doing Business Reports give a useful snapshot of a country's domestic business environment. Several of the indicators of doing business are of great relevance to international investors as well and merit attention when considering investment in a country.

Competitiveness

Probably every country in the world claims to work toward increased competitiveness, but what is actually meant by this term is not always clear. The World Economic Forum defines the term as "the set of institutions, policies and factors that determine the level of productivity of a country."[11] In practice, the elements that make up measures of competitiveness are similar to the measures of the quality of a country's business environment and therefore provide useful indicators for foreign investors.

The World Economic Forum publishes an annual Competitiveness Report,[12] covering 142 countries in its 2011–2012 edition. The report is relatively broad in scope, covering three dimensions of competitiveness (basic requirements, efficiency enhancers and innovation and sophistication factors) each of which is broken down into 12 pillars of competitiveness and are in turn based on individual scores related to more than a hundred detailed indicators. The scores along each element are made up of a combination of factual data and survey responses from local executives. The Competitiveness Report thereby contains an element of subjectivity that may be useful in the sense that perceptions often matter most in driving investment decisions. On the other hand, the report also contains some surprising results when comparing scores between countries, possibly as a result of the fact that executives are only asked about the performance of their own country in isolation. This method of scoring the elements of a country's competitiveness can make cross-country comparisons a difficult exercise.

Therefore, just as for other publications of this nature, the information presented in the report can be of great use to international companies but needs to be interpreted with care. The overall scores provide an indication of the level of competitiveness of an economy, which in turn is a major influence on the rates of return obtained on investment, the rate of economic growth and a nation's prosperity. The detailed indicator scores are useful especially as a list of factors that businesses may need to consider when investing. For example, a measure of the quality of the electricity supply may be relevant for one company, while the quality of port infrastructure may be relevant for another. In this chapter, only the overall rankings are summarized and broken down into the three main areas of basic requirements, efficiency enhancers and innovation and sophistication factors. Investors should consult the factsheets on individual countries that are under consideration as investment locations.

World Economic Forum Global Competitiveness Measures

Basic requirements: Institutions, infrastructure, macroeconomic environment, health and primary education.

Efficiency enhancers: Higher education and training, goods market efficiency, labor market efficiency, financial market development, technological readiness, market size.

Innovation and sophistication factors: Business sophistication, innovation.

Table 4.2. Global Competitiveness, 2011–2012. Rankings Out of 142 Countries

	Overall ranking	Basic requirements	Efficiency enhancers	Innovation and sophistication factors
Bahrain	37	26	31	46
Egypt	99	94	99	86
Jordan	71	61	78	70
Kuwait	34	34	67	66
Lebanon	89	109	64	78
Oman	32	20	45	44
Qatar	14	12	27	16
Saudi Arabia	17	16	24	24
Syria	98	77	109	111
UAE	27	10	25	27
Yemen	138	137	137	141

Source: The Global Competitiveness Report 2011–2012, World Economic Forum.[13]

The table shows a wide variety of competitiveness scores among the countries of the region. Just as for the World Bank's Doing Business report, the GCC countries again occupy the six top positions. With the exception of Lebanon, all countries score better on the categories of basic requirements and efficiency enhancers than on innovation. In other words, the region has been more successful in putting in place the basic requirements and infrastructure for business to operate than in building efficiency enhancers and fostering innovation. In response to this situation, several GCC countries are now making large investments to build an economy that is increasingly based on knowledge and innovation.

It is difficult to determine whether countries in the Middle East have progressed in terms of competitiveness relative to other countries. Because the number of countries covered in the report continues to increase, a certain rank in one year cannot be interpreted in the same way as the same rank in a subsequent year. Allowing for this issue, the World Economic Forum has carried out an analysis of the evolution of the Arab countries listed and concluded that overall the GCC countries have gained in competitiveness relative to the rest of the world, whereas other countries in the region have remained stable or declined slightly in relative competitiveness.

Governance Indicators

Another way of looking at a country's business environment is to consider its governance quality. Many academic studies have pointed toward the importance that international investors attach to governance issues, both at the national level and at the company level. Governance at the company level is referred to as corporate governance, a topic that will be discussed further in Chapter 6. At the country level, the term governance, which is closely linked to institutional quality, is defined by the World Bank as follows:

"The traditions and institutions by which authority in a country is exercised. This includes (a) the process by which governments are selected, monitored and replaced; (b) the capacity of government to effectively formulate and implement sound policies and (c) the respect of citizens and the state for institutions that govern economic and social interactions between them."[14]

Based on this definition, the World Bank has developed the following six worldwide Governance Indicators:

World Bank Governance Indicators

1. Voice and accountability
2. Political stability and the absence of violence/terrorism
3. Government effectiveness
4. Regulatory quality
5. Rule of law
6. Control of corruption

Although some of these items also feature in the other two reports discussed, these governance indicators are at a somewhat higher level of abstraction, providing insights into the overall functioning of a country's institutions. The worldwide Governance Indicator scores are calculated on the basis of an amalgamation of 30 public and private data sources, all of which are based on perceptions of individuals, firms and experts, for example, from Global Insight or the Political Risk Services Group. These indicators are therefore subjective in nature, but are based on a sufficiently broad set of information sources that bias of individual respondents is unlikely to be an issue. A related advantage of indicators based on expert opinion is that the scores are not based on legislation as it is in the statute books but is based on perceptions of how the legislation is implemented in practice. An alternative to using these Governance Indicators is to purchase the various governance and political risk ratings directly from an information supplier, but the World Bank indicators provide a cost-effective and easy way to start an analysis of governance quality.

The World Bank governance scores are not reported as a straightforward ranking but are instead published as a statistical analysis of the various data sources. This makes the scores not easy to interpret for the casual reader. The most recently published scores date from 2010 and since then significant developments have taken place with respect to most of the governance indicators throughout the region. For these reasons, the governance scores are not reported here, but they can easily be obtained from the relevant website (www.govindicators.org).

A high-level analysis of the most recent governance scores indicates again that the GCC countries provide a more stable business environment than other parts of the Middle East. Comparing the governance indicators with the results of the Doing Business and Global Competitiveness Reports, most countries do not score as well in terms of overall governance and political stability as they do along the measures related to the business environment and competitiveness described previously. In particular, the scores on Voice and Accountability are relatively low. The Arab Spring has provided the opportunity for Voice and Accountability to be improved in several countries in the region, but the results are as yet uncertain and improvements made to date remain fragile. Meanwhile, political stability in countries affected by the Arab Spring has actually deteriorated since the 2010 governance scores were published, at least in the short term.

The overall conclusion that the Middle East scores better in terms of business regulations and competitiveness than in terms of overall governance and political stability is one that is likely to endure. This conclusion should be kept in mind by investors who need to differentiate between a country's overall political situation and a company's ability to develop a business in a country. If an investor is able to tolerate political turmoil, it may find the most profitable opportunities in countries that have some political volatility while working to improve the business environment.

Conclusion

Understanding a country's political climate and its business and institutional environment are critical when making decisions on where and how to invest. The key for investors is not to be attracted or deterred by a country's headline performance in a ranking table, but to analyze the specific risks to a venture in a range of potential markets.

In parallel, companies can choose tools and techniques to help minimize the chances of a risk event happening and minimizing the costs when things turn bad. Although it is not possible to insure against loss of future business as a result of political factors, companies can insure against the risk of nonpayment and against expropriation risk. A number of organizations cater to companies to meet these needs, sometimes with government support from the country of the investor. Companies need to do their own risk analysis, regardless of whether such insurance is purchased because any insurance inevitably contains an element of risk sharing.

Besides insurance, the key to dealing with political and institutional risks is to engage in *flexible commitments*, by which an investor makes a serious and long-term commitment to a market but retains the operational and strategic flexibility to scale the investment up or down, or to change the structure of the investment at relatively little cost. In this way, companies can invest early and obtain an advantage over those who wait and see from the sidelines.

PART 2

Strategies for Entry and Growth

CHAPTER 5

Location Choices

The location and control decisions of multinational enterprises are at the core of managerial decision-making and academic theorising in international business.

—Buckley, Devinney and Louviere, 2007[1]

Chapters 5 and 6 deal with two critical decisions managers need to make when defining their growth strategies for the Middle East. This chapter covers location decision-making in the region, whereas the next chapter deals with decisions regarding ownership and control structures.

Many companies start getting interested in a particular market as a result of a specific opportunity, a one-off deal or a conversation with a friend or business relation. Although there is nothing wrong with capitalizing on individual opportunities, strategic location decisions benefit from a systematic analysis of the main drivers of success and an evaluation of the risks in a new market. There is no single answer on where to locate and no magic decision-making formula, but companies looking to invest in the Middle East can benefit from a thorough consideration of the factors outlined in this chapter. The actual location decision will depend on a range of company-specific factors such as the company's capabilities, financial resources and risk appetite. A second key element in location decision-making is the type of investment the company is considering. Direct international investments can be classified as market seeking, natural resource seeking or strategic asset seeking, with the focus of this chapter on market-seeking investments, that is, companies looking to market their goods and services abroad. Despite these differences in a company's circumstances, objectives and environment, there are several major decision-making criteria that all investors need to consider. These are listed below and discussed further in this chapter.

Location Decision-Making Criteria

1. Market attractiveness
2. Infrastructure
3. Quality of life
4. Taxation and cost of doing business
5. Institutions and political risk

Location Decision-Making Criteria

Market Attractiveness

For market-seeking investments, market attractiveness is clearly the critical consideration for any investor. Market attractiveness can be measured at a high level by a country's total GDP, GDP per capita and GDP growth. Demographic factors pointing toward market attractiveness include total population size, the population's age structure and population growth. For consumer goods companies, countries with a heavily urbanized population will provide the benefit of easier access to consumers than countries with mostly rural populations.

Data on the size and growth of specific markets for products and services are relatively hard to come by in emerging markets and the Middle East is no exception. National statistics agencies are still under development and market research companies are growing but are facing significant challenges in conducting meaningful research as a result of data availability issues, the multicultural composition of many Arab countries and the dynamic nature of Arab markets. After an initial, high-level analysis, a hands-on approach is therefore recommended to come to an in-depth view about a market, including its customers, competitors, suppliers and regulators.

Although there are great benefits to having a local presence, for some business-to-business activities, actual physical entry in each market may not be necessary. Instead of exporting or selling services from the company's head office or through a network of local offices, companies may establish regional operations in one location in the Middle East from which to serve the entire region. This practice has been used extensively by companies in investment banking, management consulting and other professional services. Such companies often first develop a client base in a national market and then *follow the customer* by setting up a physical and legal presence once sufficient business has been generated.

Although expanding into new markets without establishing a physical presence seems attractive from a cost point of view, there is growing reluctance among clients in the Middle East to be served by companies that do not have a local presence. In particular, companies that have set up offices in Bahrain and the UAE to serve customers in Saudi Arabia have found it increasingly useful to set up local operations. Saudi Arabia has recently started to tax companies based abroad when doing business inside the Kingdom. At the same time, the process of setting up business locally has been greatly simplified. Qatar is similarly encouraging foreign companies to set up locally. Therefore, although regional headquarters may remain in the smaller Gulf markets, at least some customer-facing staff and a legal presence are required in those large markets that are judged to be the most attractive.

Additional elements of market attractiveness that need to be taken into account are market growth and competitive intensity. Rapidly growing markets usually offer the best opportunities for new entrants. They will not only provide the promise of future growth, but these markets are also likely to have less competitive intensity and less customer bargaining power. In practice, competitive intensity is often underestimated by new entrants into the Middle East; just because the investor has not entered the market yet, it does not mean that nobody else has. As companies have targeted countries that are relatively easy to enter first, several markets are now highly competitive and may be nearly saturated for many products and services. Therefore, the so-called low hanging fruits are no longer available in most industries. The most interesting opportunities are likely to be available in the markets that may be more difficult to enter and require a greater degree of local knowledge and experience. Investors will need to balance these different factors of risk, reward and investment required when considering which markets to prioritize.

Although most available data related to market attractiveness are likely to be available only at the country level, it needs to be recognized that there are significant variations within countries and the choice of where to locate within a country can be as significant as the country choice itself. In an article titled *Is Your Emerging Markets Strategy Local Enough*, the management consulting firm McKinsey calls for a definition of strategy in the larger emerging markets at the level of regions, cities, or clusters of cities within a country. Although countries in the Middle East do not boast populations comparable to those of the BRIC nations, the article's main point of applying a *one-size-fits-all* marketing strategy has clear relevance:

> "There is no one-size-fits-all strategy for capturing consumer growth in emerging markets. What's clear, though, is that traditional country strategies and other aggregated approaches will miss the mark because they can't account for the variability and rapid change in these markets. As the battle for the wallet of the emerging-market consumer shifts into higher gear, companies that think about growth opportunities at a more granular level have a better chance of winning."
>
> *Source*: McKinsey Quarterly, April 2011[2]

In this sense, it needs to be recognized that Abu Dhabi, Dubai and the other five Emirates that make up the UAE have their own individual market characteristics. Saudi Arabia's three major regions (East, Central and West) have their own market dynamics and so do different parts of Iraq. Even smaller countries have urban and rural areas which may display significant differences in purchasing behavior, retailing structure and consumer attitudes.

The interactions between strategies at different geographic levels are demonstrated in Figure 5.1, with the corporate strategy determining the regional-level strategy which in turn determines the national and local strategies. Each level of strategy in turn influences the strategy at the level above it, so a company's Middle East regional strategy is impacted by each individual country in which the country operates and the Middle East can itself contribute to the formulation of corporate strategy.

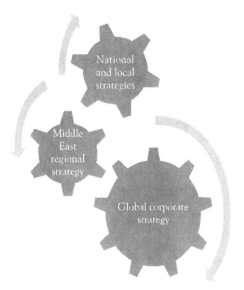

Figure 5.1. Location choice interactions.

Infrastructure

Physical infrastructure is a critical consideration in a region where the quality of infrastructure between different locations varies greatly. For many regional investors, the quality of the airport and the network of flight connections are major factors. On this dimension, Dubai stands out above the crowd, although Qatar and Abu Dhabi are also rapidly expanding their airport infrastructure as well as their international flight connections. As per the latest count, Emirates Airlines serves 120 destinations out of Dubai, Qatar Airways has 115 destinations out of Doha and Etihad has 84 destinations out of Abu Dhabi. In addition to the flights by these major carriers, many other airlines fly in and out of these regional hubs. For example, in 2010, Dubai Airport was used by 131 international airlines, thereby hosting more airlines than any major airport in the world.

A second critical element of a country's hard infrastructure is the availability of housing and office space. The supply of both types of property has increased tremendously in the last decade, leading to oversupply in some locations which in turn has helped to drive down rents.

Significant construction activity is continuing across the region to meet the anticipated growing demand for housing, offices, schools, hospitals and other types of infrastructure.

A third infrastructure element to consider is the quality and cost of telecommunications. Competition in the telecoms sector is somewhat limited and controlled in most Middle Eastern countries, leading to relatively high prices by global standards. Some small businesses complain they pay nearly as much in telecom costs in rent.

Quality of Life

Quality of life considerations are of great importance for companies looking to have an international workforce in their foreign operations. Quality of life is a very personal matter and people will have their own preferences as to what they consider a good place to live. Depending on the profile of the staff a company wishes to attract, factors to be considered include the country's safety, availability of international schools, entertainment possibilities, community life and the cost of living. Companies should take quality of life into consideration not from the perspective of a single person or small group of individuals, but rather from the perspective of the general profile of people the company is looking to staff the company with in the medium term. In this way, a resignation of a key member of staff will be easier to deal with.

There are a number of corporate functions for which companies tend to have a choice of where to locate, regardless of where the market activity takes place. Such functions include regional headquarters, back-office operations and call centers. For these geographically mobile activities, quality of life can be an important consideration for location decision-making, although locations with an attractive quality of life for expatriates may be less attractive from a cost point of view.

Taxation and the Cost of Doing Business

Although tax considerations such as corporate tax, income tax and value added or sales tax usually play an important role in choosing investment locations, in the Middle East the issue needs to be viewed in the context of the overall cost of doing business. Taxes in the Middle East are generally very low by Western standards and some countries are *tax free* in the sense that they do not levy any income or corporate tax. In practice, all countries do raise some taxes, with even GCC countries charging import duties and operating a sales tax for at least some goods and services. Still, if location decisions were made based on taxes alone then nearly every country in the region would be an attractive proposition, with the GCC nations coming out on top. However, there are other related cost factors that play a role in the location decision-making process.

First, all governments do need to raise revenue regardless of their oil wealth and they have identified various ways of doing so without necessarily introducing taxes in the strict sense of the word. Costs for licenses, electricity, telecommunications and property differ greatly between locations, with a substantial part of any profit of these operations accruing to the government in one way or another (either directly or through dividend payments from government-controlled companies). Many investors have learned too late that the cost of business is substantially higher than expected after all these relevant fees and costs have been taken into account.

Second, as the taxation base is low, the level of government provision of certain services is also naturally low, at least for expatriates. This is particularly true for healthcare and education, where investors looking to employ expatriate staff need to make their own arrangements and need to include the associated costs in their budgets. Expatriates are also not provided with social security or retirement benefits and need to make their own provisions for these matters. In many countries, a company contribution to retirement is mandated by the government through the payment of a gratuity benefit equivalent to one month's salary for each year of service, payable when the employment contract ends.

In summary, investors need to look beyond the headline tax rates and rent levels of a location and build a more complete and integrated picture of their cost profile when making location decisions.

Institutions and Political Risk

The quality of a country's institutional environment and the political risk level are key determinants in location decision-making, particularly in the Middle East where these factors often raise concerns among investors. Chapter 5 has provided an overview of the institutions and risk profiles of Middle Eastern countries. Although it is self-evident that good institutions and low risk are preferable, it is not always the case that countries with high risk and poor institutions have to be avoided. Institutions and risk are just one factor to be considered and need to be put into the context of the overall investment opportunity. Case studies of multinational companies with extensive experience in the Middle East[3] have shown that political instability is not a reason to avoid markets if the market attractiveness is high enough. These experienced investors see political risk as an inherent feature of the region and treat it as a risk to be accepted and dealt with rather than a risk to be avoided at all cost. Some companies see their ability to deal with political risk as an important competency and a source of competitive advantage. According to the case studies, only when there is a risk to the security of the company's employees do foreign investors avoid direct investment in a particular country.

In the same case studies, it was pointed out that investors do take political risk and institutions into account when deciding on the location of regional headquarters. Regional headquarters or regional hubs can be established anywhere regardless of the location's market potential and during the last decade many companies have chosen to locate their regional hubs in the relatively small market of Dubai. Previously, Beirut and Bahrain have been regional centers, particularly for financial services companies. The Lebanese Civil War prompted banks to leave Beirut in the 1980s and more recently companies have shifted their operations from Bahrain to Dubai in response to the political developments there. Regional hubs are more mobile than local country operations and are therefore more sensitive to political risk.

The Decision-Making Process

The location decision criteria described in the preceding section provide a general framework for making location choices. In practice, a company may take additional factors into account and every company will attach a different weight to each of the individual criteria depending on its unique circumstances. A company's preferences for specific locations will be influenced by factors such as its size, risk profile and experience in the region. An investing company will therefore first clarify its own decision-making criteria and investment objectives at the start of its evaluation.

Companies can make location decisions as an iterative process whereby first a large number of countries are evaluated very quickly, followed by a more in-depth assessment of the two or three most attractive locations. Visits by senior executives then become critical in order to come to a proper assessment of the suitability of a location. At this stage in the process, a company can contact its own Consulate as well as the Foreign Investment Promotion Agency in the locations that are under serious consideration. Foreign Investment Promotion Agencies vary widely in the region in terms of their sophistication and support provided to foreign investors. Their most likely role is that of an information provider and facilitator of contacts. In some cases, these agencies may also be able to negotiate incentives for specific investment projects, such as the use of land or tax benefits. In recent years, Saudi Arabia's SAGIA has been the most prominent example of an investment agency taking a structured and proactive approach, with significant results. In the UAE, foreign investment promotion is not carried out at the Federal level but at the level of the individual Emirate. Several countries have a long-standing Investment Promotion Agency, whereas some other countries may have recently established agencies. Each country covered in this book now has at least one agency that is a member of the World Association of Investment Promotion Agencies (WAIPA) and the contact details of each of these agencies can easily be found on WAIPA's website (www.waipa.org).

Conclusion

The topics discussed in this chapter are intended to provide a general framework for location decision-making for market seeking investments in the Middle East. In the end, location decisions are based on many factors that are specific to the market, the company and the type of investment under consideration. These factors make location decision-making a process that involves both judgment and analysis.

CHAPTER 6

Entry and Operation Modes

Experience builds a firm's knowledge of a market, and that body of knowledge influences decisions about the level of commitment and the activities that subsequently grow out of them.
> —Jan Johanson and Jan-Erik Vahlne, 2009[1]

Together with location choices, decisions on entry and operation mode arrangements are considered to be the most critical in a company's international expansion strategy. An entry mode refers to the institutional arrangement chosen by a company when entering a market. Entry modes can be classified along a continuum that ranges from low through medium to high levels of equity and control (see Figure 6.1). As the foreign company invests more equity in a given operation, it accepts a greater share of the business risk in return for a higher level of control and a higher share of the returns. Exports are the entry mode which represent the lowest form of control, followed by licensing arrangements and franchising. Medium control modes include joint ventures, whereby the equity in a local company is shared between the foreign investor and a local company. High-control entry modes essentially consist of wholly owned subsidiaries.

In the context of entry modes, there are two additional concepts that are relevant: operation modes and establishment modes. The term *operation mode* refers to a company's institutional arrangement at any given moment in time, whether at the moment of entry or afterwards. As circumstances change, companies may adapt their structures to the new realities and change, for example, from a licensing arrangement to a joint venture or a wholly-owned subsidiary. In such cases, it is said that they operate under an operation mode that is different from their original entry mode choice.

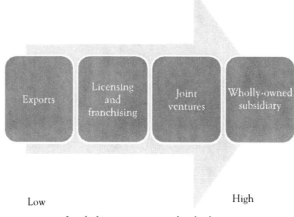

Low   High

Level of investment, control and risk

Figure 6.1. Entry and operation mode choices.

Second, a company's *establishment mode* refers to the way in which an entry mode choice is realized, that is, does the company enter through a greenfield operation or through acquisition? Both joint ventures and wholly-owned subsidiaries may be obtained either through a greenfield investment, whereby the company establishes its own operations, or through an acquisition, where the company takes over all or part of the equity of an existing operation. The establishment mode of acquisitions is the subject of Chapter 7.

Choices regarding entry and establishment modes and the continuous management of a company's operation modes are critical management responsibilities that can contribute or detract greatly from a company's profitability. If the right choices are made at the start, then the ongoing management of a country's operation mode does not demand much management attention. However, if an inappropriate mode is selected, particularly if a company chooses an inappropriate partner to deal with, management can spend as much time on partnership renegotiations as on the actual business itself. Even if the correct choice is made initially, managers need to review the appropriateness of their structure in the light of changes to legislation, the competitive environment, or the company's internal circumstances.

How Companies Make Entry Mode Choices

There is a vast amount of academic literature published on the complex subject of entry mode choices. A range of characteristics of companies, countries and industries combine to provide a number of competing explanations on how companies make entry mode decisions. It is difficult to generalize about entry mode choices, because such decisions are based on a large number of considerations, including external factors (e.g., legislation, competitive environment), internal factors (company preferences, international experience and strategic considerations) as well as chance (e.g., the availability of an appropriate partner or acquisition candidate in the target market). This section will briefly discuss some of the main drivers of entry mode choices, particularly in the context of the Middle East. For this purpose, the investments to be made are assumed to be market seeking, that is, the foreign company is looking to enter a country in search for markets, regardless of whether these markets consist of consumers, businesses, or government. This type of investment is in contrast with resource-seeking investment as found, for example, in the natural resources sector.

As mentioned in the previous chapter, for market-seeking investments, market size and growth are critical factors in attracting investor interest. Generally speaking, the larger a market, the easier it will be for a company to justify an equity investment, thereby favoring high-equity entry modes in large and rapidly growing markets. An additional factor that determines market attractiveness is competitive intensity. If a market is already characterized by very intensive competition, a foreign company will tend to prefer to serve it via exports initially. Oligopolistic markets, with less intense competition, offer a greater profit opportunity and a greater need for an equity investment by a foreign company. Therefore, each of the main determinants of market attractiveness point toward equity investments being more prevalent in highly attractive markets.

Another consideration that has been at the center of academic explanations of entry mode decisions is that of transaction costs. This concept refers to the costs of carrying out a transaction on the open market compared with keeping it within the hierarchy of the company. In principle, companies are expected to prefer to leverage their skills, brand name and resources as much as possible and to contract out their operations in foreign markets. This is exactly what companies relying on franchising such as McDonald's and Starbucks have done worldwide. The restaurant company maintains a focus on product design, marketing and the supply chain, while a local operator actually runs the outlets.

However, in many cases the costs of concluding and monitoring contracts with outside parties are such that it becomes more attractive for companies to carry out their own activities abroad. This may be the case if there is a concern over opportunism (or cheating) on the side of the foreign partner and concern over the enforceability of contracts between the partners. Such concerns may arise for various reasons. First, the foreign investor may want to ensure that its intellectual property is not used by another company in unintended ways. This is particularly the case if the knowledge shared between the investor and the local partner is not easily codifiable, that is, when there is tacit knowledge. Second, when the foreign investor is concerned over its brand name and reputation, it may be reluctant to let other parties act on its behalf. This issue is generally not much of a concern in industries such as retailing or restaurants, where contracts can more easily provide adequate provisions of how a brand name should be used. However, businesses that are more closely tied to the individuals who perform the service, such as banking, consulting and other professional services, usually prefer to have business carried out in its name only by the company's own employees, over whom the company has full hierarchical control. A third example of transaction cost considerations is when a local licensee may have objectives that are different from the international investor. For example, a local player will try to maximize local profitability from any particular customer, whereas the global company may accept losses on one customer in one country if these are made up for with profits on the same customer in other markets. Such conflicting objectives are difficult to resolve if the international investor does not have full control over its local operating company. These and other transaction cost considerations motivate many companies to control their foreign operations.

A complementary view to the transaction costs approach is offered by the internalization process school,[2] which argues that companies with little international experience enter a market through exports and progressively move toward operation modes with higher degrees of control, as their skills and experience in working in the foreign market increase. The additional international experience that a company builds up over time reduces uncertainty for the foreign investor and makes them more willing to invest in higher equity operation modes in order to increase control over the venture. In this way, international experience is seen as an element that reduces risk for the company and allows it to step up its investment. Although this argument for a step-by-step approach is appealing, it needs to be set against the switching costs that companies incur when changing from one operation mode to another. Although moving from exporting to a licensing or joint-venture agreement looks like a natural and relatively easy step to make, moving from licensing to joint venture or from a joint venture to full ownership can be complicated and costly, particularly if it involves altering or severing the links with a well-established local partner.

Various external risk factors will also have an effect on entry mode decisions. For example, high levels of political risk in a country will increase uncertainty associated with a foreign market entry and will typically make companies less willing to invest, encouraging them to choose low-equity entry modes. As a company gains experience in assessing and mitigating political risk in the context of its business in the region, it will be more willing to take on such risk, if the returns are sufficiently attractive. Research on the entry mode decisions of multinational companies in the Middle East has shown that experienced international investors do not shy away from high-risk markets, unless there is a physical security risk to the company's employees.[3] These investors often take political risk into account through the discount rate which they use to estimate the Net Present Value of a foreign investment project. In this way, the forecasted cash flows associated with an investment in a foreign market are discounted by a discount rate that reflects all the risks associated with the project, including the political risks. Although it is difficult to come to a good view of how much the discount rate should be increased by as a result of political risk, the underlying principle is valid as investors expect to be compensated for taking on additional risk by a higher expected investment return.

An analysis of these and other external risk factors results in the conclusion that companies are less likely to invest in a foreign market through a high-equity mode of entry if there is a high risk associated with the investment. In such cases, exports or a form of licensing or franchising are often preferred, until the company has built up sufficient experience and knowledge of dealing with the risks in the particular market or the risk profile of a country changes.

Entry Mode Options in the Middle East

The entry mode choice in the Middle East is a complex one and the factors described above only represent some of the main considerations to take into account, rather than a complete formula for decision-making. The following sections describe the different entry mode options available to companies in the context of the Middle East region.

Wholly-Owned Subsidiaries

Based on the consideration described in the previous section, a company may prefer to retain full ownership of its operations in the Middle East. If this is the case, it is important to be aware that there are various restrictions placed on foreign ownership of companies in the region, depending on the country and industry sector of the investment. In practice, all countries in the world place some restrictions on foreign ownership of companies, especially in industrial sectors that are considered sensitive in one way or another. In the Middle East, such restrictions are generally stricter than in Western markets, but they are evolving quickly as the benefits of FDI become clearer and competition among countries to attract international investors heats up. Since the Asian crisis of 1998, many emerging economies have started to see FDI as a more stable way of generating foreign currency than portfolio investments, which may be withdrawn at the touch of a button. These days, even the oil-rich countries that have no immediate need for foreign currency have realized the important spillover benefits that FDI can generate. Such benefits from FDI include skills transfer, employment opportunities and an acceleration of the diversification of the economy. As a result, countries in the Middle East have generally been relaxing the restrictions placed on foreign ownership. In the GCC, Bahrain, Saudi Arabia and Qatar all allow full foreign ownership in at least some industry sectors.

Oman, Kuwait and the UAE are also in the process of liberalizing their foreign investment legislation. Elsewhere, Lebanon, Jordan and Egypt have traditionally been more open to foreign investment and have placed fewer restrictions on foreign ownership.

In this dynamic context, it is worthwhile for investors to understand not only the current possibilities for full ownership but also to try to anticipate future legislative developments. Although such developments depend on political factors and are therefore by nature unpredictable, an assessment can be made of likely trends. Given the increasing pressure on Middle Eastern governments to ensure there are employment opportunities for their young and growing populations, it is a reasonable expectation that most countries will continue to open up their economies in order to attract foreign investment.

The judgment that remains to be made is if and when full foreign ownership will become possible in the relevant sector and how much this matters to the international investor. For example, in Saudi Arabia, several financial service companies have entered into joint-venture arrangements at a time when full foreign ownership was not an option. Now that Saudi Arabia has allowed full foreign ownership for certain types of financial service companies, some investors may now wish they had waited until the full ownership option became available, particularly because switching out of a joint venture can be problematic. On the other hand, some companies may be well satisfied with their joint-venture arrangements and companies that entered the market early will benefit from first-mover advantages.

In countries where majority ownership of companies is not possible in onshore locations, there is often the possibility of establishing in a free zone. Free zones are created with the express purpose of facilitating foreign companies to set up and to provide them with the option of full ownership. Investors in free zones generally benefit from clear regulations and strong support from the free zone organization when setting up their business. The free zone commercial regulations may be different from a country's *mainland* regulations and different free zone regulations in one country may also have different regulations from each other. In countries with many free zones, such as the UAE, free zones often specialize in a particular sector, such as logistics, finance, media, education, information technology, or industry. There has been a rapid growth in the number and size of free zones over the last decade, as countries have been seeking to make their locations attractive to foreign investors without necessarily changing the overall investment legislation.

Although the legal environment under which companies in free zones operate will differ between individual free zones, the following description of the legal environment applicable to Dubai-based free zones is typical for free zone operations throughout the region.

Dubai Free Zones

The free zones in Dubai were established for the specific purpose of facilitating foreign investment and therefore were given distinct legal status in the UAE. Legal entities incorporated and operating within the free zones are not subject to many of the restrictions imposed by UAE Federal Law concerning Commercial Companies as well as other UAE laws and regulations.

Entities operating within a free zone may be 100% foreign owned and are permitted to distribute profits to shareholders and/or a parent company even if the same resides in a foreign country. Free zone entities benefit from a Dubai government undertaking that they will not be subject to taxes for a specific period of time (...) In addition, free zone entities are also exempt from all import duties.

Although the free zones are based in Dubai, companies operating within free zones are treated as being offshore or outside the UAE for legal and operational purposes. As a result, limitations exist on the business activities of free zone entities outside of the relevant free zone, as a free zone licence will not permit the free zone entity to carry on its activities outside of its free zone into the general UAE jurisdiction.

In order to sell its products and provide its services throughout the Emirate of Dubai, the respective free-zone entity must appoint a locally licensed commercial agent or distributor. Accordingly, free zones are suitable for companies intending to use Dubai as a regional manufacturing, distribution or service base particularly in circumstances where a large part of their business is based outside the UAE.

Source: Hadef & Partners, company website (www.hadefpartners.com).

In August 2011, FDI Intelligence (part of the Financial Times) published a ranking of the top 25 free zones in the Middle East, based on criteria of economic potential, incentives, facilities, cost effectiveness, transportation and promotion. Out of 130 participants, an expert panel of judges came up with a ranking of the top 25 free zones in the region.

Middle East North Africa Free Zone Ranking

1. Dubai Airport Free Zone	United Arab Emirates
2. RAKIA Industrial Park	United Arab Emirates
3. Jebel Ali Free Zone	United Arab Emirates
4. RAK Free Trade Zone	United Arab Emirates
5. Abu Dhabi Airport Free Zone	United Arab Emirates
6. Jubail New Industrial City II	Saudi Arabia
7. Tangier Exportation Free Zone	Morocco
8. Dubai Internet City	United Arab Emirates
9. Dubai Media City	United Arab Emirates
10. Dubai Knowledge Village	United Arab Emirates
11. Bahrain International Investment Park	Bahrain
12. Aqaba Special Economic Zone	Jordan
13. Dubai International Financial Centre	United Arab Emirates
14. KADDB Industrial Park	Jordan
15. Mafraq Development Zone	Jordan
16. (KAEC) King Abdullah Economic City	Saudi Arabia
17. Salalah Free Zone	Oman
18. Dubai International Academic City	United Arab Emirates
19. Sharjah Airport International Free Zone	United Arab Emirates
20. Hamriyah Free Zone	United Arab Emirates
21. Dubai Healthcare City	United Arab Emirates
22. Dubai Outsource Zone	United Arab Emirates
23. Dead Sea Development Zone	Jordan
24. Qatar Science and Technology Park	Qatar
25. International Media Production Zone	United Arab Emirates

Source: FDI Intelligence. Middle East Fee Zones of the Future 2011/2012.

Free zones have many attractions including a clear regulatory frame-work, no taxes (although the free zone does charge its own licensing fees and rents) and the possibility of full ownership. However, for companies looking to serve clients inside the country in which the free zone is located, a free zone is rarely the final answer. In addition to a free zone location, in most cases trade with local customers will need to be carried out by legal entities with an onshore location in the relevant country.

If neither a wholly-owned subsidiary nor establishment in a free zone are possible, a company may maintain control over its operations through a tie up with a local partner in an arrangement that is a joint venture on paper but enables the foreign company to run the business on a day-to-day basis. In these cases, the role of the local partner (a *silent partner*) is limited to administrative matters such as licensing and visa applications for foreign staff. In some cases, the local partner will provide business development support by arranging introductions to decision makers in the country and act as a general liaison between government authorities and the investor. Some people in Gulf countries specialize in providing this type of service to foreign investors and entertain a large number of joint-venture partners in a range of industries. Although these arrangements can work effectively for a long time, it needs to be recognized that the foreign investor does remain dependent on the local partner, who is still the majority owner of the company. If relations between the parties turn sour for any reason there can be significant risks for the foreign investor. On occasions, government authorities have also voiced their dissatisfaction with these structures, although so far no specific government actions have been taken against the operation of such service arrangements.

Joint Ventures

In principle, joint ventures in the Middle East work much like they do across the world. Like anywhere else, joint ventures work best if there is a clear and true partnership that bundles the complementary capabilities of different firms. There are, however, a number of region-specific considerations that need to be taken into account. First, as described in the previous section, in several countries the foreign partner to a joint venture is not allowed to have a majority stake in the joint venture if the business is registered outside a free zone. This limits the ability of foreign companies to maintain majority control or even to have 50/50 partnerships.

Second, it needs to be kept in mind that in the Middle East a local company may have joint-venture arrangements with a number of competing multinationals. This is particularly the case in the retail sector, where a local conglomerate (sometimes also acting as a shopping mall developer and operator) may represent a large number of competing brands. In such cases, the foreign company provides its brand and products to the venture, whereas the local partner provides local retailing expertise and access to prime shopping mall locations. This arrangement raises the question of which foreign company's wishes get priority in case of conflicting interests between several foreign partners of a single local distributor. In practice, although multinationals will need to monitor that the local partner adequately represents the interests of the joint venture, there is no significant evidence of major conflicts that arise from these situations.

A final point to take into account when dealing with joint-venture partners in the region is the question of who represents the partnership in dealing with local authorities. If the local company is the majority owner of the venture, then it can be expected that it will deal with licensing and other regulatory issues. Recently, companies with operations in the US or the UK have become vigilant about compliance with their national corruptions legislation, the US Foreign Corrupt Practices Act and the UK Briberies Act, respectively. These regulations put limits on the so-called political partnerships and force companies to take their own responsibility for representing themselves to foreign governments. As a result, foreign investors need to make sure that they are not misrepresented in communication with host government authorities and that there are no payments made which may conflict with the anticorruption legislation of the US or the UK. These conditions apply not only to companies headquartered in the US or the UK, but also to all companies with operations in these countries.

Licensing and Franchising

Licensing and franchising work much the same way in the Middle East as they do elsewhere. The market for franchising is well developed, with a wide range of franchising consultants offering services and a number of national and regional franchising fairs taking place each year. These fairs give franchisors the opportunity to make contact with possible franchisees across the region. Many of the major franchises of large fast food chains, coffee shops, or retail stores are already taken up, in some cases by large family owned companies who hold the rights for several countries for one brand. However, the market is very dynamic and new opportunities arise on an ongoing basis.

Exports

Exports are sometimes not regarded as a market entry mode, because the exporting company is not required to establish any operation in its target market. This is particularly the case for indirect exports, where a local agent or distributor will represent the foreign company. Exports are a form of entry that entails relatively low risk and low commitment. For most products, some adaptation and translation will need to be made to the packaging and the product information, but in many cases one set of adaptations will suffice for the whole region. Exports can provide an important learning experience for foreign companies, which can subsequently develop into a physical presence.

In the case of services provided to consumers (restaurants, hotels, banking), a physical presence is required from the start. However, professional service providers may first serve a market from abroad, fulfilling contracts for individual business customers before opening an office in the market. This way of operating allows a foreign service provider to postpone investment until it is clear that an attractive market exists. However, there is growing reluctance among users of professional business services to deal with these *suitcase bankers* and unless there is a relatively unique service on offer, clients will prefer to work with suppliers who have a physical presence in the market.

Conclusion

On paper, all entry and operation modes are available to international investors throughout the region, although there are important restrictions to full foreign ownership in some countries. Practical decisions on entry modes need to be made in the context of a company's capabilities, resources, risk profile and strategy and with reference to the locally applicable regulations. Although legislative developments are difficult to predict, an assessment needs to be made of existing regulations as well as of potential changes in legislation. This is important because operation modes that involve a partnership arrangement are difficult to change. Therefore, joint ventures and local partners need to be seen as more than just a necessary step to comply with current local legislation and need to be based on a genuine combination of complementary skills and assets between parties that know and trust each other.

Although a step-by-step approach to increasing a company's commitment to a market makes intuitive sense, in practice many companies are now party to licensing and joint-venture agreements that are costly to change.

CHAPTER 7

Mergers and Acquisitions

The delta between a good deal and a bad one is much bigger than in developed markets. If things go well, investors stand to make a lot of money. But if things go badly, investors can lose big.
—PricewaterhouseCoopers, Getting on the Right side of Delta,
A dealmaker's guide to growth economies[1]

When companies enter a new market and establish operations through either a joint-venture arrangement or a wholly-owned subsidiary, there are two establishment modes they can employ: greenfield entry or acquisitions. Greenfield entry refers to the building up of a new operation from scratch, for example, by purchasing or building of new facilities. On the other hand, acquisitions refer to the purchase of one company by another company. The terms greenfield and acquisitions are not only relevant for initial market entry; once a company has entered the region, it may expand into other markets or consolidate its position through further greenfield investments or through acquisitions of existing companies.

Although true mergers are rare in the Middle East, commentators use the term M&A for merger and acquisitions activity and this chapter will also use the two terms M&A and acquisitions interchangeably. Following a big drop in M&A activity after the boom years of 2007 and 2008, M&A volumes have recently held up relatively well in the Middle East. Information publisher Zawya entitled its report on M&A activity for the first half of 2011 *Shrugging off the Effects of the Arab Spring*. The actual volume and value of M&A deals reported differ between various information sources. Ernst & Young puts the value of M&A transactions for 2011 at US $31.7 billion (down from

US $44.1 billion in 2010) and the volume of deals at 416 (up from 401 in 2010). The average value of deals continues to fluctuate, going down during 2011 and rising again in early 2012. As a relatively small market for M&A activity, overall transaction values and average deal values in the region can depend significantly on the absence or presence of a few large acquisitions.

There are strong indications that investors continue to find acquisition opportunities even during times of political upheaval. The more stable markets of Saudi Arabia, Qatar and the UAE have the highest level of activity, although some investors have also taken advantage of lower company valuations in Egypt. In terms of industry sectors, the telecommunications, real estate, financial services and energy sectors have historically dominated M&A activity. These industries are likely to see continued M&A activity as consolidation is now taking place at a regional level. In addition, deals are now also materializing in other sectors including technology and media. The large amount of Private Equity that has been raised during the last decade in the region is leading to full or partial acquisitions, which in turn will be available for sale once a Private Equity company seeks to exit from its investment. The companies looking for growth capital or facing succession issues provide further impetus for renewed growth in mergers and acquisition activity.

Entry or growth through acquisitions provides many potential benefits to international investors, principally in terms of the reduced time it can take to buy a company compared with building up an operation from scratch. At the same time, acquisitions are accompanied by a series of risks and challenges that need to be managed. This chapter discussed the particular challenges that foreign acquirers face in the Middle East and suggests ways of dealing with them.

A summary of considerations regarding greenfield entry versus entry through acquisitions is provided in Figure 7.1.

The remainder of this chapter deals with each of the steps in the acquisition process: searching for acquisition targets, determining value and negotiating and integrating the acquired company. A final section of the chapter deals with corporate governance considerations.

Greenfield	Acquisition
Opportunity for step-by-step development	Opportunity for fast entry
Certain resources and capabilities may be difficult to acquire (e.g., talent, locations)	Can provide unique resources and capabilities
Add to competitive landscape	No additional competitors as result of entry
Entrant needs to comply with local regulations	Acquisition may not be possible for foreign entities
Investment may benefit from government incentives	Cash flow or succession issues may provide opportunities for acquisition
	Valuation and negotiation challenges
Implementation challenges	Integration challenges

Figure 7.1. Greenfield development versus acquisitions.

Scanning for Potential Acquisition Candidates

Identifying potential acquisition targets is not an easy exercise in the Middle East. Although stock markets can point toward opportunities for acquisition, the region's stock markets are relatively small and are dominated by companies in a small number of sectors, particularly finance, construction, property and telecommunications. Other important sectors in the region's economy such as retail, consumer goods, tourism, logistics and transport are usually privately owned and companies for sale are more difficult to identify and evaluate. As potential acquisition targets, stock market-quoted companies are rarely for sale in their entirety, either because of foreign ownership limits or because significant minority shareholders (either government entities or families) are not looking to sell the entire company. For these reasons, hostile takeovers by foreign companies are, practically speaking, not possible in the region, with the rare exceptions usually involving a bidder from within the region. Quoted companies can still be of interest to multinational companies as they may have divisions or country operations which parent companies may be willing to divest as part of a corporate restructuring. In this sense, the global economic slowdown may offer new opportunities for foreign investors as many companies in the Middle East are now keen to raise cash and focus on their core activities. This restructuring trend is likely to endure as broadly-based conglomerates start to become more selective and concentrate on a more limited scope of business activity, selling peripheral assets to raise funds for expansion in core sectors.

Besides divisions of quoted companies, the large number of unquoted companies provides the main source of potential acquisition candidates. As a starting point, some type of market study will need to be carried out in order to assess both the attractiveness of different markets and to identify potential partners or acquisition candidates. Such research is useful even if an entrant is not looking to make an acquisition, because acquisition targets are most likely to be competitors if a company enters through a greenfield investment.

The identification of potential partners or takeover targets can be facilitated by professional service firms. Although the region is well served by global investment banks, management consultants, corporate lawyers and accounting firms, many of the well-established service providers focus on the top end of the market and are less keen on assisting companies with medium-sized transactions. This leaves a gap in the middle end of the market, which is slowly being filled by a set of newer and smaller service providers. With or without external support, an acquirer will usually draw up a long list of potential acquisition candidates, including divisions of larger companies and progressively narrow the list down through research and analysis. Trade exhibitions and business news websites (as listed in the appendix) can be useful sources of information to identify players in an industry. Once a manageable number of companies remain on the list, an initial approach can be made to the owners of the company to inquire if a sale or another type of transaction or cooperation is possible.

In the process of acquiring companies in the Middle East, it is essential to keep in mind that the vast majority of companies are family owned and are in practice run as family companies. This may provide opportunities as many owner managers are currently looking to retire and sell the company if their younger family members are not interested to continue running the business. At first sight, it may appear as if buying a family-owned company is relatively simple, because there is only the owner manager to deal with and decision-making should be relatively straightforward. In reality, buying a family company can get complicated, with various constituencies playing a role in the decision-making process that the buyer may not immediately be aware of. For family-owned companies, a disposal is just one option of dealing with succession issues and an acquisition process will inevitably become a part of a wider discussion on succession among family members. This can make the negotiation process lengthy, thereby negating some of the advantages of acquisitions as a quick method of market entry.

Determining Value and Negotiating

Determining the value of an acquisition target is a challenge in any environment and particularly so in the Middle East. Requirements to publicly file financial accounting information are virtually nonexistent for companies that are not quoted on the stock market. This makes it difficult for potential buyers to understand the financial performance of a company before having contact with the owners. Even if the owners do provide financial information, the level of detail and accuracy may not always be what acquirers need. In countries without corporate taxation (principally the GCC countries), there is no financial incentive to be conservative in financial accounting when drawing up the company's profit and loss account. As a result, the financial statements may in some cases inflate the performance of a company. Although this situation can make an assessment of a company's current performance more difficult, it does have the potential advantage of forcing an acquirer to think deeply about what benefits an acquisition would bring. Because it will usually not be possible to simply take the target's historic accounts and extrapolate the financial performance using some assumptions on growth, an acquirer needs to consider what capabilities the acquisition brings to the table and how these can translate into synergies and future profits. Such an analysis may include, with the permission of the current business owner, discussions with key stakeholders such as customers, suppliers and employees to determine how they might react to a change of ownership. In this way, determining the value of an acquisition, if done properly, becomes an exercise in business planning and should be dealt with as such. As per traditional business planning and investment valuation techniques, the exercise ends with estimates of the future cash flows of the acquired business, which are then discounted at a rate that reflects the riskiness and the cost of capital of the project. The resulting present value of the cash flows of the business is equivalent to the value of the target for the buyer.

As mentioned, the Middle East region is characterized by high growth and high levels of political risk. This makes estimating the future cash flows of a company and using the appropriate discount rate in valuation purposes a difficult exercise. Future cash flows of a target may be much higher or lower than at the time of acquisition, depending on market conditions as well as factors such as how successfully the acquirer can integrate its capabilities with the target company. Cash flows may be further impacted by political risk events, such as changes in legislation or political turmoil. Some investors reflect political risk in the discount rate with which acquisition projects are evaluated, with cash flows of projects in more risky countries being discounted at a higher rate. Other companies plan a range of scenarios, attach a probability to each one and multiply the cash flows of each scenario with the anticipated likelihood of the scenario materializing. Whichever method is used, an analysis of the political and regulatory environment of the target company is an essential component of any acquisition decision.

Given the high level of uncertainty when estimating the future cash flows of an acquisition target, negotiation skills become critical in obtaining a good outcome. One of the reasons for the lack of growth in the M&A market in the region is the so-called valuation gap, with current owners putting a much higher valuation on the company than potential buyers. Many owners still seem to have pre-2008 valuations in their mind and refuse to take account of the new realities. In these cases, acquisitions are not materializing despite the presence of a strong logic to work out a deal.

The valuation gap arises because potential buyers and sellers often have widely differing views about the future cash flows of a business and hence about its value, particularly if the business contains a large share of intangible assets, such as reputation and customer relationships. One critical assessment to make in the valuation exercise is whether these intangible assets are reduced or increased in value when the company ownership changes hands.

In addition to the uncertainty about future cash flows, the valuation gap occurs because there are usually few comparable deals in order to benchmark a particular transaction. Western analysts will quickly be able to point at comparable *price/earnings ratios* or typical *price to book ratios* in their home markets, but in the Middle East it is unlikely that there have been several recent transactions that are in any way comparable to the one under consideration. Even for deals that do materialize, the transaction value is often not disclosed. This makes the benchmarking of valuations extremely difficult. As a result, even if there is broad agreement on the potential future profitability of the target, it is not clear how to place a value on these future profits. In Discounted Cash Flow terminology, a seller will tend to perceive the business risk as much lower than a potential buyer, thereby attaching a higher value to future profits than a buyer would.

It is generally advisable not to speak about price early in the negotiation process. Family owners may be as concerned about leaving the company in good hands as they are about maximizing value. Sellers may also be concerned about the position of remaining family members or loyal staff who are to remain in the company. Talking about money too quickly may inhibit the relationship building that is required for a successful takeover. The buyer may also find out more information about the target during the early discussions, which will help to adjust the estimated value of the company. The field of negotiations and how to deal with cultural differences is the subject of a number of books in its own right and will not be dealt with in detail here. Suffice to say that local knowledge is the key. The target company should be analyzed in all its dimensions, including its management, customers, suppliers and competitors. This is not only critical when negotiating but is also an important element in planning a successful post-acquisition integration.

Integration Challenges

Once a transaction for the purchase of a company is completed, the process of creating value begins. Whether a company is purchased as a stand-alone investment or as part of the acquirer's existing activities in the region, the buyer will look to improve the performance of the acquisition target. In this process, it is worth remembering that cultural issues are quoted as the most common reason for acquisition integrations to fail, with potential cultural issues relating to both national and company culture. Without going into the details of acquisition integration or cultural management here, it is clear that any integration approach must be based on careful planning and a high level of knowledge of and respect for the cultures represented in the company.

Specific consideration also needs to be given to the role of existing management in the newly combined companies. In many cases, the owner of family-controlled companies holds key relationships with clients, suppliers, employees and government authorities which need to be maintained. A continuing involvement of previous management may smooth relations with these stakeholders, but may also cause confusion. Generally speaking, if the acquirer has its own client relations and a set of systems and processes that the acquisition target can fit in to, and if the acquirer has experience of operating in the region, then the need for previous management to stay on for an extended period of time diminishes.

Integration challenges are one reason why acquisitions by foreign companies in the region are relatively rare. Most recent acquisitions have been either by local players or by private equity firms. A merger or acquisition between two local players, for example, in the banking or construction sector, provides immediate opportunity for cost reduction through the elimination of overlap between the two companies. Investment by a local private equity company often starts with a minority stake and provides the investor with the opportunity to inject fresh capital and management skills in order to take a rapidly growing company to the next level. Yahoo!'s acquisition of Maktoob in 2009 has been seen by many as a landmark deal which may herald more acquisitions by Western companies. The Maktoob deal has been followed up by

Coke's December 2011 acquisition of around half of Saudi Arabia's Aujan group for US $980 million.

Yahoo! Buys Maktoob

One of the most high-profile foreign acquisitions in the region has been Yahoo!'s acquisition of Maktoob in August 2009. Although the value of the deal has not been disclosed, some reports suggest that Yahoo! paid around US$ 75 million for the Arabic language internet portal.

The Financial Times[2] reported: "The deal's relatively small size belies its significance. A new generation of entrepreneurs and companies are starting to make their mark on the region's corporate landscape—and further afield."

Maktoob was started by Jordanian alumni of Anderson Consulting in 2000 as a free e-mail service, but has rapidly grown into a news, financial information, and internet services portal that reaches a combined 16.5 million monthly users across the Middle East. "The future of Arab entrepreneurship will be known as Before Maktoob–Yahoo and after Maktoob–Yahoo," wrote Fadi Ghandour, an Arab businessman and an early investor in the company, on Twitter soon after the event.

Maktoob is now fully integrated into Yahoo!.

Corporate Governance

Corporate governance considerations are important in the context of mergers and acquisitions for a variety of reasons. First, an acquirer will want to know that it can rely on the financial information published by the target company and that its decision-making processes regarding the acceptance of an offer to buy the company are in line with international standards. Second, both banks and financial market participants who are asked to be involved in financing an acquisition will want to be assured that both buyer and seller of the target company operate on the basis of international corporate governance standards before committing any funds. More broadly, the enforcement of good corporate governance standards is essential for the development of a country's banking sector and the functioning of financial markets, which in turn are needed to attract investment and help to grow the economy.

From being a relatively unknown concept in the region 10 years ago, corporate governance has developed to become a major topic in public and private companies alike. The historic lack of attention to corporate governance is due to the traditional preference for privacy, the reluctance of family owners to relinquish control and the limited role of securities markets compared with traditional bank finance. In 2005, an OECD (Organization for Economic Co-operation and Development) report described the status of corporate governance in the context of mergers and acquisitions as follows:[3]

> "Most family companies in the MENA are characterised by a strong family leader. Not surprisingly, families play also an important role in shaping boards of directors, by nominating family members, close relatives or senior managers. Evidence also suggests that the higher the ownership share of the dominant family shareholder, the more likely it is for the chief executive officer to be a member of that family. This leads to tight oversight of management by the family with little role for the board. Family and other controlling shareholders influence corporate decisions also indirectly through their stakes in a number of holding companies and subsidiaries. Under such circumstances the market for corporate control is not very active throughout the region. In spite of stronger disclosure provisions and other legal improvements to ensure that mergers and acquisitions are conducted in an orderly fashion and with due respect to minority shareholder rights, their number has only modestly increased in recent years. It is also worth noting that many appear to be related to corporate restructuring and rescue plans."

Corporate governance has developed a great deal since then. Today, whether a company seeks finance from banks or through the capital markets, the providers of capital are taking a range of corporate governance issues into account. Common corporate governance considerations include the independence of the Board of Directors and their effectiveness in monitoring management, the treatment of minority shareholders and the provision of correct and complete and timely information on the company's financial performance. A 2011 report from the OECD entitled *The Second Corporate Governance Wave in the Middle East and North Africa* provides an updated view of the situation:

> "The end of this decade marks the end of the first corporate governance wave in the region, and it is undeniable that it has brought tangible results. Corporate governance, or *hawkamah* in Arabic, is no longer a term that needs defining, nor is its business case unclear. Even from a family business perspective, the case for better governance needs less justification today than it did only five years ago. This is not to deny that market regulators and stock exchanges across the region continue to face challenges in enticing family-owned companies to list their equity. The reluctance of family-owned firms to open their equity to outside shareholders is perhaps a key factor stifling corporate growth and further development of the region's capital markets."[4]

The OECD report describes two waves of improvements in corporate governance practices. The first wave consisted of the definition and publication of voluntary codes in nearly all Middle Eastern countries. The second wave is currently under way and is all about making good corporate governance mandatory and improving legal enforcement of proper standards. Efforts to improve corporate governance are being made by a variety of players, including government agencies, stock markets and other private sector bodies. Several countries now have their own institute dealing with corporate governance issues, with the Dubai-based Hawkamah Institute for Corporate Governance the most active at the regional level.

Still, corporate governance standards vary widely between companies in the region and the issue is of great relevance to both portfolio investors and direct investors. Companies with good corporate governance are not only more transparent during an acquisition process, but they are also likely to be more professionally managed and less volatile.

Conclusion

Entry or growth through acquisition is potentially a quick way to expand in the region. Although acquisitions are always accompanied by significant risk, a number of actions can be taken to mitigate against these risks. Acquirers who do their homework, remain patient and treat sellers respectfully are most likely to succeed. Investors also need to make sure they manage the acquisition as a continuous process from opportunity identification through to deal making and integration. With these provisos in mind, the Middle East is likely to offer many opportunities of growth through acquisitions, as conglomerates restructure and family-owned companies are working on management succession.

Given the particular characteristics of companies, capital markets and legislation in the region, foreign investors need to give serious consideration to buying minority stakes in companies as a potential first step to full ownership. Minority stakes provide the opportunity to limit a company's financial commitment and risk and allow for a learning process that can be used to make subsequent investments on a sound basis of knowledge and experience.

CHAPTER 8

Implementation Considerations

This chapter contains seven important practical considerations in the context of defining and implementing market entry and growth strategies in the Middle East. The advice provided here takes the preceding chapters one step further in order to help managers to avoid making the mistakes that have been made by others before. Not all recommendations provided should be followed blindly in all circumstances; however, they do provide important guidelines.

Middle East Strategy Implementation Considerations

1. Accept and manage political risk
2. Flexible commitment
3. Avoid an early exit
4. Build true partnerships
5. Hire local staff
6. Ensure documentation
7. Respect culture

1. Accept and Manage Political Risk

Successful investors have accepted that the level of political risk in the Middle East is inherently higher than elsewhere and that there is no point in waiting for regional stability to arrive before entering or expanding in the region. Within a regional business plan, individual country strategies may differ as a result of political risk factors. Some of the most unstable countries may be avoided or given a lower priority, especially if there is a security risk to staff. However, even recently volatile countries such as Iraq may have regions where risk is more manageable and opportunities are significant. The most stable countries can serve as regional entry points and as regional hub locations. Medium risk countries may be entered once sufficient regional knowledge and experience have been built up. As outlined in Chapter 4, different companies will be affected in different ways by various types of political risk and a country-level analysis is required to determine which risk factors are of most concern to the particular investment under consideration.

Various actions can be taken to manage the consequences of political risk. Trade credit insurance companies can help to mitigate against payment risk as a result of either the default of the company's customer or of political circumstances preventing payment. The World Bank's Multilateral Investment Guarantee Agency (MIGA) provides political risk insurance to investors. The types of risk covered by MIGA's guarantees include currency inconvertibility, expropriation, war, terrorism, breach of contract and the nonhonoring of sovereign financial obligations.

2. Flexible Commitment

Any business book will tell managers to be both committed and flexible when going about their work. In the context of entry strategies in the Middle East, these terms have a specific meaning. First of all, companies must make a real commitment to the markets in which they want to succeed. Building relationships with potential customers take time and can hardly be done during occasional visits to a country. Customers in the region are now looking for solutions that are specific to their local circumstances and people flying in from Europe to share so-called best practices are finding it increasingly necessary to tailor their offering. In order to succeed, companies are more and more required to have a physical and legal presence in each market.

Flexibility comes into play when a company must respond to changing circumstances. One such change may be the relaxation of restrictions on foreign ownership or other changes to a country's commercial legislation. Under these circumstances, companies benefit from not being completely locked into a set of arrangements from which it is very costly to change.

Such arrangements may include partnership agreements, employment contracts, licenses, or property leases that seemed appropriate upon market entry and are later found to be difficult to get out of. Currently, many companies in the region operate in locations or operation modes that under the current circumstances they would not choose, but switching costs prevent them from changing to a set up that would suit them better.

3. Avoid an Early Exit

When a company decides to completely withdraw from a market it will often find it extremely difficult to return at a later stage. Personal relations are of paramount importance in the Middle East and the local business community and regulators will always remember which investors remained committed to a market during difficult times. A prime example of this is Lebanon, where many people will be able to say exactly which foreign banks remained open during the country's long civil war.

The difficulties of re-entering a market are well illustrated by Citibank's effort to get back into Saudi Arabia:

> Citigroup aims to open for business in Saudi Arabia six years after selling its stake in a bank there. However the bank is discovering that returning to the Saudi market might not be as easy as departing. Since leaving the country in 2004, the company has said it would like to regain a foothold.

> "The franchise that Citibank led in Saudi Arabia was very robust and prosperous for many years and they decided at that point to exit," said Riyadh's Banque Saudi Fransi chief economist John Sfakianakis.

> A year later, Mohammad Al Shroogi, the Middle East managing director, called the exit a *mistake* and said the bank was reapplying for a license to operate.

> "The central bank, the Saudi Arabian Monetary Agency (SAMA) has temporarily halted the issuance of new bank licenses in order to evaluate the many licenses issued so far," he said.[1]

If a company has good reasons to reduce its financial commitment to a market, it should at least maintain a legal presence, including the required licenses to operate and a skeleton staff. On such a basis, it will be much easier to expand again once the business environment improves.

4. Build True Partnerships

A foreign investor can benefit greatly from partnering with a local company with complementary capabilities. Local partners are often able to provide local clients and suppliers, access to prime property and are able to help the foreign investor navigate his way through a set of country-specific circumstances, customs and legislation.

In countries where full foreign ownership is permitted, foreign investors should still seriously consider linking up with a local partner in order to enhance the chances of success and to leverage the investor's financial commitment and capabilities.

In countries and sectors where full or majority foreign ownership is not possible, investors must be careful not to conclude a joint venture just because it is a legal requirement to do so. Agreements with so-called silent partners effectively pay the local partner an annual fee to allow the foreign company to operate, while maintaining full management and operational control with the foreign investor. These agreements work well when there are no financial or legal issues on either the side of the local partner or the foreign investor, but when one of the parties gets into difficulty, such agreements can break down acrimoniously.

Finally, partnerships must be based on complementary business capabilities and not on political liaisons. Political partnerships can get international companies into trouble with the US Foreign Corrupt Practices Act or the UK Bribery Act, which stipulate that there should be no partnerships based on political connections to a host country government. In any case, it has been demonstrated in recent years that those with political power and connections in the Middle East may change suddenly and locking oneself into an equity-sharing arrangement because of a person's political connections alone may leave a foreign company empty handed when political circumstances change. If a company needs help in navigating through a country's regulations and needs to build a better understanding of government buyers, it is usually preferable to obtain these insights through a consultancy agreement rather than a sharing of ownership.

5. Hire Local Staff

There are both demand and supply considerations that make it imperative for companies operating in the Middle East, particularly the Gulf region, to hire more local staff than they have done up to now.

With the rapid growth of the local labor force, improvement in education levels and the fact that government jobs are increasingly hard to obtain, hiring local staff is now easier than before. Hiring local staff is also a cheaper way of obtaining local expertise and potential business contacts than consultancy contracts and it provides more flexibility than a joint-venture arrangement. If an employee does not perform, there are ways of dealing with the situation. If a joint-venture partner does not live up to expectations, it all gets more complicated.

Western universities now graduate large numbers of Arab speakers who can be effective managers for companies operating outside or inside the Middle East. In many cases, Arab graduates are recruited into a company in the US or Europe where they start their careers. After several years in the company's home market operations, they can return to their country of origin at a senior level and act as an effective bridge between the Middle East country operation and the rest of the company. Local universities also increasingly turn out highly qualified-bilingual graduates in a variety of disciplines who can be recruited on campus. Well-managed internships are a particularly effective way for a company to get familiar with prospective employees.

The benefit of hiring local staff manifests itself at all levels, from junior staff needing to speak Arabic with customers and suppliers, to senior management and country-level board members needing to network with senior clients and government representatives. Soon companies will not have a choice about recruiting local employees as Gulf governments are becoming more serious about sanctions and incentives to encourage the nationalization of the workforce. It is much better to be proactive about hiring local staff and see it as a business opportunity rather than as a cost of doing business. Nearly every company that has made a serious effort in growing its local workforce has done very well out of it.

6. Ensure Documentation

The great importance of personal relations when doing business in the Middle East should not be mistaken for a lack of relevance for proper documentation in all of a company's dealings. The 2008 economic crisis has made it clear that when there are difficulties or ambiguities about getting paid, only formal and proper documentation regarding agreements, purchase orders, work completion forms and extensions of contracts are acceptable, regardless of what the foreign party may think has been agreed verbally. In this sense, the Middle East is no different from other markets, but investors should not be confused about this point when dealing with business partners on a personal level. The same concern applies to partnership arrangements described in Section 4 of this chapter. As everywhere, when difficulties and disagreements arise, what is signed on paper will be the main basis for any arbitration that is used to resolve the conflict.

7. Respect Culture

This book has not gone into the details of cultural considerations and business etiquette, even though many business failures in the region have been attributed to the challenges associated with different cultures working together. The keys to successfully dealing with cultural issues are knowledge and attitude.

In terms of knowledge on Middle Eastern cultures, Geert Hofstede's national culture dimensions provide a useful framework. Hofstede has grouped several countries together and displays the average scores for four cultural dimensions on his website (www.geert-hofstede.com). The scores can then be compared with the country of the investor. For example, in comparison to the US, the Arab region scores high on the dimensions of Power Distance and on Uncertainty Avoidance, low on Individualism and a slightly lower score on Masculinity (referring to the importance of competition, achievement and success). Analyzing such scores for the country in which a foreign company is looking to invest can be a useful starting point to understanding culture.

There are specialist books available on the topic of culture in the Middle East with titles including the words *Culture shock!*, *Culture smart!* and *Don't they know it's Friday?*[2] Such books can provide useful information for newcomers into the region and can accelerate the learning process about a country, but in all cases this information needs to be complemented with a respectful attitude and real experience of a country's culture. A respectful attitude to cultural differences involves an awareness of the ways of working with others and avoiding an ethnocentric approach in doing business. Experience of a country's culture can be built up by interacting with the local population and by sharing experiences with fellow foreign investors and expatriates.

Conclusion

As a final note, companies are advised to be both ambitious and patient when entering or expanding in the region. The emerging markets of the Middle East offer tremendous opportunity for investors. Given the challenges and risks that the execution of any growth strategy will bring, any investment in terms of time and money is only going to be worthwhile if a company sets its goals high and remains patient and committed in the face of temporary setbacks.

Appendix

Country Profile: Bahrain

Population (2010)	1.3 million
Population (2050)	2.0 million
Gross domestic product	US $22.7 billion
GDP per capita	US $20,475
Area	620 km^2
Top 3 trading partners (Exports)	Saudi Arabia, Qatar, India
Top 3 trading partners (Imports)	European Union, Brazil, China
Doing Business—global ranking (2012)	38
Global competitiveness ranking (2012)	37
Share of world oil reserves	—
Share of world gas reserves	—
Inward Foreign Direct Investment stock (2010)	US $15,154 million
Inward Foreign Direct Investment flow (2010)	US $156 million
Outward Foreign Direct Investment stock (2010)	US $7,883 million
WTO/OPEC membership	WTO

Country Profile: Egypt

Population (2010)	80.4 million
Population (2050)	137.7 million
Gross Domestic Product	US $218.5 billion
GDP per capita	US $2,789
Area	1,001,450 km^2
Top 3 trading partners (Exports)	European Union, Saudi Arabia, United States
Top 3 trading partners (Imports)	European Union, United States, China
Doing Business—global ranking (2012)	110
Global Competitiveness Report—ranking (2012)	99
Share of world oil reserves	0.3%

(Continued)

Share of world gas reserves	1.2%
Inward foreign direct investment stock (2010)	US $73,095 million
Inward foreign direct investment flow (2010)	US $6,386 million
Outward foreign direct investment stock (2010)	US $4,272 million
WTO/OPEC membership	WTO

Country Profile: Iraq

Population (2010)	31.5 million
Population (2050)	64.0 million
Gross Domestic Product	US $82.5 billion
GDP per capita	US $2,619
Area	437,072 km^2
Top 3 trading partners (Exports)	Syria, Jordan, Iran
Top 3 trading partners (Imports)	n/a
Doing Business—global ranking (2012)	164
Global Competitiveness Report—ranking (2012)	n/a
Share of world oil reserves	8.3%
Share of world gas reserves	1.7%
Inward foreign direct investment stock (2010)	US $6,487 million
Inward foreign direct investment flow (2010)	US $1,426 million
Outward foreign direct investment stock (2010)	—
WTO/OPEC membership	OPEC

Country Profile: Jordan

Population (2010)	6.5 million
Population (2050)	11.8 million
Gross Domestic Product	US $27.5 billion
GDP per capita	US $4,500
Area	92,300 km^2
Top 3 trading partners (Exports)	Iraq, United States, India
Top 3 trading partners (Imports)	European Union, Saudi Arabia, China
Doing Business—global ranking (2012)	96
Global Competitiveness Report—ranking (2012)	71

(Continued)

Share of world oil reserves	—
Share of world gas reserves	—
Inward foreign direct investment stock (2010)	US $20,406 million
Inward foreign direct investment flow (2010)	US $1,704 million
Outward foreign direct investment stock (2010)	US $483 million
WTO/OPEC membership	WTO

Country Profile: Kuwait

Population (2010)	3.1 million
Population (2050)	5.4 million
Gross Domestic Product	US $131.3 billion
GDP per capita	US $36,412
Area	17,820 km²
Top 3 trading partners (Exports)	China, UAE, Saudi Arabia
Top 3 trading partners (Imports)	n/a
Doing Business—global ranking (2012)	67
Global Competitiveness Report—ranking (2012)	34
Share of world oil reserves	7.3%
Share of world gas reserves	1.0%
Inward foreign direct investment stock (2010)	US $6,514 million
Inward foreign direct investment flow (2010)	US $81 million
Outward foreign direct investment stock (2010)	US $18,676 million
WTO/OPEC membership	WTO, OPEC

Country Profile: Lebanon

Population (2010)	4.3 million
Population (2050)	5.0 million
Gross Domestic Product	US $39.2 billion
GDP per capita	US $10,044
Area	10,400 km²
Top 3 trading partners (Exports)	European Union, Switzerland, United States
Top 3 trading partners (Imports)	European Union, United States, China
Doing Business—global ranking (2012)	104

(Continued)

Global Competitiveness Report—ranking (2012)	89
Share of world oil reserves	—
Share of world gas reserves	—
Inward foreign direct investment stock (2010)	US $37,040 million
Inward foreign direct investment flow (2010)	US $4,955 million
Outward foreign direct investment stock (2010)	US $7,150 million
WTO/OPEC membership	None

Country Profile: Oman

Population (2010)	3.1 million
Population (2050)	5.4 million
Gross Domestic Product	US $55.6 billion
GDP per capita	US $18,657
Area	212,460 km²
Top 3 trading partners (Exports)	UAE, India, China
Top 3 trading partners (Imports)	UAE, European Union, China
Doing Business—global ranking (2012)	49
Global Competitiveness Report—ranking (2012)	32
Share of world oil reserves	0.4%
Share of world gas reserves	0.4%
Inward foreign direct investment stock (2010)	US $15,196 million
Inward foreign direct investment flow (2010)	US $2,045 million
Outward foreign direct investment stock (2010)	US $2,228 million
WTO/OPEC membership	WTO

Country Profile: Palestinian Territories

Population (2010)	4.0 million
Population (2050)	9.4 million
Gross Domestic Product	US $5.8 billion
GDP per capita	US $1,367
Area	5,898 km²
Top 3 trading partners (Exports)	n/a
Top 3 trading partners (Imports)	n/a

(Continued)

Doing Business—global ranking (2012)	131
Global Competitiveness Report—ranking (2012)	n/a
Share of world oil reserves	—
Share of world gas reserves	—
Inward foreign direct investment stock (2010)	US $1,551 million
Inward foreign direct investment flow (2010)	US $115 million
Outward foreign direct investment stock (2010)	US $1,644 million
WTO/OPEC membership	None

Country Profile: Qatar

Population (2010)	1.7 million
Population (2050)	2.6 million
Gross Domestic Product	US $129.5 billion
GDP per capita	US $76,168
Area	11,437 km^2
Top 3 trading partners (Exports)	Japan, Korea, India
Top 3 trading partners (Imports)	n/a
Doing Business—global ranking (2012)	12
Global Competitiveness Report—ranking (2012)	14
Share of world oil reserves	1.9%
Share of world gas reserves	13.5%
Inward foreign direct investment stock (2010)	US $31,428 million
Inward foreign direct investment flow (2010)	US $5,534 million
Outward foreign direct investment stock (2010)	US $25,712 million
WTO/OPEC membership	WTO, OPEC

Country Profile: Saudi Arabia

Population (2010)	29.2 million
Population (2050)	49.8 million
Gross Domestic Product	US $443.7 million
GDP per capita	US $16,996 million
Area	1,960,582 km^2
Top 3 trading partners (Exports)	Japan, Taipei Chinese, United States

(Continued)

Top 3 trading partners (Imports)	European Union, United States, China
Doing Business—global ranking (2012)	12
Global Competitiveness Report—ranking (2012)	17
Share of world oil reserves	19.1%
Share of world gas reserves	4.3%
Inward foreign direct investment stock (2010)	US $170,450 million
Inward foreign direct investment flow (2010)	US $28,105 million
Outward foreign direct investment stock (2010)	US $16,960 million
WTO/OPEC membership	WTO, OPEC

Country Profile: Syria

Population (2010)	22.5 million
Population (2050)	36.9 million
Gross Domestic Product	US $59.3 billion
GDP per capita	US $2,877
Area	185,180 km²
Top 3 trading partners (Exports)	European Union, Iraq, Lebanon
Top 3 trading partners (Imports)	European Union, Russia, China
Doing Business—global ranking (2012)	134
Global Competitiveness Report—ranking (2012)	98
Share of world oil reserves	0.2%
Share of world gas reserves	0.1%
Inward foreign direct investment stock (2010)	US $8,715 million
Inward foreign direct investment flow (2010)	US $1,381 million
Outward foreign direct investment stock (2010)	US $418 million
WTO/OPEC membership	None

Country Profile: United Arab Emirates

Population (2010)	5.4 million
Population (2050)	9.4 million
Gross Domestic Product	US $301.9 billion
GDP per capita	US $59,717
Area	78,000 km²

(Continued)

Top 3 trading partners (Exports)	Taipei Chinese, India, Iran
Top 3 trading partners (Imports)	European Union, India, China
Doing Business—global ranking (2012)	33
Global Competitiveness Report—ranking (2012)	27
Share of world oil reserves	7.1%
Share of world gas reserves	3.2%
Inward foreign direct investment stock (2010)	US $76,175 million
Inward foreign direct investment flow (2010)	US $3,948 million
Outward foreign direct investment stock (2010)	US $55,560 million
WTO/OPEC membership	WTO, OPEC

Country Profile: Yemen

Population (2010)	23.6 million
Population (2050)	52.2 million
Gross Domestic Product	US $31.3 billion
GDP per capita	US $1,282
Area	527,970 km^2
Top 3 trading partners (Exports)	China, India, Thailand
Top 3 trading partners (Imports)	European Union, UAE, China
Doing Business—global ranking (2012)	99
Global Competitiveness Report—ranking (2012)	138
Share of world oil reserves	0.2%
Share of world gas reserves	0.3%
Inward foreign direct investment stock (2010)	US $4,196 million
Inward foreign direct investment flow (2010)	—
Outward foreign direct investment stock (2010)	US $513 million
WTO/OPEC membership	None

Notes

Chapter 1

1. Wagstyl (2011).
2. Van Agtmael (2007).
3. Population Reference Bureau (2010).
4. United Nations Statistics Division (2011).
5. International Monetary Fund (2012).
6. Khanna and Krishna (2010).
7. Van Agtmael (2007).
8. The term *Next Eleven* originates from Jim O'Neill of Goldman Sachs and includes 11 large and promising emerging markets other than the BRIC countries: Bangladesh, Egypt, Indonesia, Iran, Mexico, Nigeria, Pakistan, Philippines, South Korea, Turkey and Vietnam.

Chapter 2

1. International Monetary Fund (2012).
2. The International Bank for Reconstruction and Development/The World Bank (2012).
3. International Monetary Fund (2012).
4. BP Statistical Review of World Energy (2011).
5. Kalkman, Nordin and Yahia (2007).
6. Ezzine, Thacker and Chamlou (2011).
7. Ezzine, Thacker and Chamlou (2011).
8. See, for example, Aguirre, Cavanaugh and Sabbagh (2011).
9. Simpfendorfer (2009).
10. *Financial Times* (2009).
11. Nazim and Ibrahim (2011).
12. Population Reference Bureau (2010).

Chapter 3

1. Van Agtmael (2007).
2. Ramamurti and Singh (2009).
3. Sauvant, Govitrikar and Davis (2011).
4. Fortune Global 500 (2011).

5. Forbes (2012).
6. Verma et al. (2011).
7. Verma et al. (2011).
8. Wagstyl (2011).
9. Verma et al. (2011).
10. *The Economist* (2010a).
11. Emirates (2010).

Chapter 4

1. International Monetary Fund (2012).
2. Khanna and Krishna (2010).
3. Root (1994), pp. 130–132.
4. The International Bank for Reconstruction and Development/The World Bank (2012).
5. The International Bank for Reconstruction and Development/The World Bank (2012).
6. *The Economist* (2010b).
7. The International Bank for Reconstruction and Development/The World Bank (2012).
8. Arabian Business (2011).
9. The International Bank for Reconstruction and Development/The World Bank (2011).
10. Hawkamah (2009).
11. World Economic Forum (2011).
12. World Economic Forum (2011).
13. World Economic Forum (2011).
14. Kaufmann, Kraay and Mastruzzi (2010).

Chapter 5

1. Buckley, Devinney and Louviere (2007), pp. 1069–1094.
2. Atsmon, Kertesz and Vittal (2011).
3. Rogmans (2011).

Chapter 6

1. Johanson and Vahlne (2009), pp. 1411–1431.
2. Johanson and Vahlne (2009).
3. Rogmans (2011).

Chapter 7

1. Dwyer et al. (2012).
2. Wigglesworth (2009).
3. OECD (2005).
4. Koldertsova (2010).

Chapter 8

1. Arabian Business (2010).
2. Williams (2010).

References

Aguirre, D., Master Cavanaugh, M., & Sabbagh, K. (2011). The future of women leaders in the Middle East. Issue 63.

Arabian Business (2010). *Bringing it all back home.* Retrieved from: http://www.arabianbusiness.com/bringing-it-all-back-home-201565.html

Arabian Business (2011). *Dubai widens jurisdiction of DIFC courts.* Retrieved from: http://www.arabianbusiness.com/dubai-widens-jurisdiction-of-difc-courts-428085.html?tab=Videos

Atsmon, Y., Kertesz, A., & Vittal, I. (2011, April). Is your emerging market strategy local enough? *McKinsey Quarterly.*

BP Statistical Review of World Energy June 2011. (2011). London: BP.

Buckley, P., Devinney, T., & Louviere J. (2007). Do managers behave the way theory suggests? A choice-theoretic examination of foreign direct investment location decision-making. *Journal of International Business Studies 38,* 1069–1094.

Dwyer, J., Rimmer, A., Page, N., Skinner, R, Duval, W., & Davies, C. (2012). *Getting on the right side of delta: A dealmaker's guide to growth economies.* London: PricewaterhouseCoopers.

Emirates (2010). Subsidy. The myths and facts about Emirates and our industry. Retrieved from: http://www.emirates.com/iq/arabic/images/201004291050_Subsidy_The%20myths%20and%20facts_tcm477-557688.pdf

Ezzine, M., Thacker, S., & Chamlou, T. (2011). An exception to the gender gap in education: the Middle East? World Bank MENA, Knowledge and Learning Quick Note Series, Issue 41.

Financial Times (2009, December 15). *Chinese trade flows along new 'Silk Road'.* Retrieved from: http://www.ft.com/intl/cms/s/0/c9a93230-e8d4-11de-a756-00144feab49a.html#axzz22CU4I8lD

Forbes (2012). *Global 2000 leading companies.* Retrieved from: http://www.forbes.com/lists/2012/18/global2000_2011.html

Fortune Global 500 (2011). Retrieved from: http://money.cnn.com/magazines/fortune/global500/2011/full_list/

Hawkamah (2009). *Survey on insolvency systems in the Middle East and North Africa.* Dubai, UAE: Hawkamah Institute for Corporate Governance.

International Monetary Fund (2012, April). *Regional economic outlook: Middle East and Central Asia.* Washington, DC: International Monetary Fund.

Johanson, J., & Vahlne, J. (2009). The Uppsala internationalization process model revisited: From liability of foreignness to liability of outsidership. *Journal of International Business Studies 40,* 1411–1431.

Kalkman, J., Nordin, L., & Yahia, A. (2007, February). Moving energy intensive industries to the Gulf. *McKinsey Quarterly*. New York.

Kaufmann, D., Kraay, A., & Mastruzzi, M. (2010). The worldwide governance indicators: Methodology and analytical issues. World Bank Policy Research Working Paper, No. 5430.

Khanna, T., & Palepu, K. G. (2010). *Winning in emerging markets: A road map for strategy and execution*. Boston, MA: Harvard Business Press.

Koldertsova, M. (2010). The second corporate governance wave in the Middle East and North Africa. *Financial Market Trends 9*(2), 219–226.

Nazim, A. M., & Ibrahim, I. (2011). *The world Islamic banking competitiveness report*. Dubai, UAE: Ernst & Young.

OECD (2005). Advancing the corporate governance agenda in the Middle East and North Africa: A survey of legal and institutional frameworks. MENA OECD Investment Program Working Group.

Population Reference Bureau (2010). *2010 World population data Sheet*. Washington, DC: Population Reference Bureau.

Ramamurti, R., & Singh, J. V. (eds.) (2009). *Emerging multinationals in emerging markets*. New York: Cambridge University Press.

Rogmans, T. (2011). *The determinants of foreign direct investment in the Middle East North Africa region*. PhD Thesis, Nyenrode Business Universiteit. Breukelen

Root, F. R. (1994). *Entry strategies for international markets*. San Franciso, CA: Josey-Bass.

Sauvant, K. P., Govitrikar, V. P., & Davis, K. (2011). *MNEs from emerging markets: New players in the world FDI market*. New York: Vale Columbia Center on Sustainable International Investment.

Simpfendorfer, B. (2009). *The new silk road: How a rising Arab world is turning away from the West and rediscovering China*. New York, NY: Palgrave MacMillan.

The Economist (2010a, 3 June). Commercial aviation: Super-duper-connectors from the Gulf. *The Economist*, print edition.

The Economist (2010b, 4 November). Business and bureaucracy: Snipping off the shackles. *The Economist*, print edition.

The International Bank for Reconstruction and Development/The World Bank (2011). '*Doing business in the Arab World*'. Washington, DC: The International Bank for Reconstruction and Development/The World Bank.

The International Bank for Reconstruction and Development/The World Bank (2012). *Doing business in a more transparent world*. Washington, DC: The International Bank for Reconstruction and Development/The World Bank.

United Nations Statistics Division (2011). *World Statistics Pocketbook*. New York: United Nations Statistics Division.

Van Agtmael, A. (2007). *The emerging markets century*. New York, NY: Free Press.

Verma, S., Sanghi, K., Michaelis, H., Dupoux, P., Khanna, D., & Peters, P. (2011). *Companies on the move: Rising stars from rapidly developing economies are reshaping global industries.* 2011 BCG Global Challengers. Boston, MA: The Boston Consulting Group.

Wagstyl, S. (2011, August 14). Compelling reasons to increase engagement. *Financial Times.*

Wigglesworth, R. (2009, September 9). Gulf: Ambition usurps domestic focus. *Financial Times.*

Williams, J. (2010). *Don't they know it's Friday? Cross-cultural considerations for business and life in the Gulf.* Dubai, UAE: Motivate Publishing.

World Economic Forum (2011). *The global competitiveness report 2011–2012.* Geneva, Switzerland: World Economic Forum.

Useful Websites

www.ameinfo.com	Middle East business news
www.arabianbusiness.com	Middle East business news
www.ask-ali.com	UAE guide, including culture and etiquette
www.bayt.com	Recruitment website
www.doingbusiness.org	Doing Business reports
www.fdiintelligence.com	Foreign Direct Investment information and analysis
www.geert-hofstede.com	Insights into national cultures
www.govindicators.org	World Bank governance indicators
www.hawkamah.org	Hawkamah—the Institute for Corporate Governance
www.miga.com	Multilateral Investment Guarantee Agency
ww.waipa.org	World Association of Investment Promotion Agencies
www.weforum.org	World Economic Forum—Global Competitiveness Report
www.zawya.com	Middle East business news

About the Author

Tim Rogmans is assistant professor at the College of Business at Zayed University in Dubai, United Arab Emirates, where he teaches courses in strategy, economics, and management. He previously worked in the United Kingdom, France, and the Netherlands as strategy consultant for LEK Consulting and Gemini Consulting, and as senior manager for Atradius Credit Insurance. In 2005, he moved to Lebanon where he taught at the Hariri Canadian University. In 2007, he joined Zayed University as manager of the university's executive education unit and then joined the College of Business faculty in 2010. His research work is in the areas of international business, strategy, and corporate governance. Tim Rogmans has carried out training and consulting projects throughout the Middle East for both local and international organizations. He holds a Bachelor's degree from the London School of Economics, an MBA from INSEAD, and a PhD from Nyenrode University.

Index

A
Arab graduates, 101
Arab Middle East countries, 4
Arab speakers, 101
Arab Spring, 1, 8, 16, 57
Arab women, 20
Asian crisis, 76
Asset light model, 39

B
Bilateral Investment Treaties (BITs), 46
Boston Consulting Group (BCG), 34
Business regulations, improvement of, 14–18

C
Companies, Middle East in, 73–76
Competitiveness, 53–55
Corporate governance, 93–96
Country's
  hard infrastructure, 65
  mainland regulations, 77
Culture, respect, 102

D
Decision-making process, 68–69
Demographics, 27–30
DIFC
  courts, 51
  insolvency framework, 52
Discounted Cash Flow terminology, 91
Documentation, 102
Doing Business
  cost of, 66
  indicators, 50
  report, 48, 49, 53, 55
Dubai duty free, 40
Dubai free zones, 78

E
Early exit, 99
Emerging multinationals, 35–36

Emirates airlines, 41–42
Emirates, 41
Energy reserves, 19
Energy resources, 18–20
Entry and establishment modes, 72
Entry and operation modes
  companies, 73–76
  entry mode options
    exports, 82
    joint ventures, 80–81
    licensing and franchising, 81
    wholly-owned subsidiaries, 76–80
Entry mode choice, 7, 76
Entry mode options, 76
Equity-sharing arrangement, 100
Eroding buffers, 19
Establishment mode, 72
Etihad airways, 36, 42
Euro crisis, 25
Exports, 82
Expropriation risk, 46

F
Failed states, 3
Family-owned company, 89, 92
Flexibility, 98
Flexible commitment, 58, 98
Foreign direct investment (FDI), 3, 15
Foreign Investment promotion agency, 69
Foreign ownership, 100
Free zones, 77–81
Future cash flows, 90

G
Geert Hofstede's national culture dimensions, 102
Global economic crisis, 25, 52
Governance
  indicators, 55–57
  ownership, 36
  support, 39–40

Green buildings, 27
Greenfield entry, 85–87
Gulf common currency, 23
Gulf cooperation council (GCC)
    countries, 7, 21, 22, 24, 26,
    30, 50, 55, 57, 67, 89
Gulf Monetary Union, 25

I
Implementation considerations
    culture, respect, 102
    documentation, 102
    early exit, 99
    flexible commitment, 98
    local staff, 101
    political risk, 97
    true partnerships, 100
Infrastructure, 65
Institutions and political risk, 67
Institutions and risk
    competitiveness, 53–55
    governance indicators, 55–57
    regulatory environment, 48–53
    risk analysis, 47
Integration challenges, 92–93
Intraregional variations, 7–9

J
Joint ventures, 80–81

L
Lebanese Civil War, 68
Licensing and franchising, 81
Local labor force, 101
Local licensee, 74
Local partner, 80, 100
Local staff, 101
Location advantages, 37
Location choices
    decision-making process, 68–69
    location decision-making criteria
        doing business, cost of, 66
        infrastructure, 65
        institutions and political
            risk, 67
        market attractiveness, 62–65
        quality of life, 66
        taxation, 66

M
Maktoob, 93
Market attractiveness, 62–65
MENASA (Middle East North Africa
    South Asia), 38
Mergers and acquisitions
    corporate governance, 93–96
    integration challenges, 92–93
    potential acquisition candidates,
        87–89
    value determination, 89–91
Middle East consumers, 26
Middle East economies, 2–5
Middle East megatrends
    demographics, 27–30
    energy resources underpin growth,
        18–20
    improving business regulations,
        14–18
    political instability, 14–18
    regional integration, 23–25
    turning east, 22–23
    value-based consumption,
        26–27
    women, rise of, 20–22
Middle East multinationals, 36, 38
Middle East North Africa (MENA),
    8, 21, 26, 38, 52
Middle East North Africa free zone
    ranking, 79
Middle East strategy, 97
Middle East, emerging
    intraregional variations, 6–9
    Middle East economies, 2–5
    opportunity, 9–10
Multilateral Investment Guarantee
    Agency (MIGA), 98
Multinational companies
    emerging multinationals, 35–36
    Emirates airlines, 41–42
    strategies, 36
        government support, 39–40
        location advantages, 37
        no legacy, 36
        operational excellence, 38

N
No legacy, 36

O
OECD (Organization for Economic Co-operation and Development), 94
Oil and gas reserves, 20
Oil reserves, 18–20
Oil-rich middle eastern countries, 2
Oligopolistic markets, 73
One-size-fits-all marketing strategy, 64
Operation mode, 71
Operational excellence, 38
Operations risk, 46
Organization of the Petroleum Exporting Countries' (OPEC) members, 7

P
Pan-Arab channels, 24
Peak oil, 18
Political
    instability, 14–18
    partnerships, 100
    risk, 97
Political, economic, social, technological, legal and environmental (PESTLE), 13
Potential acquisition candidates, 87–89
Potential partners, 88

Q
Qatar airways, 36, 42, 65
Quality of life, 66

R
Regional integration, 23–25
Regulatory environment, 48–53
Risk analysis, 47

S
Saudi Arabia General Investment Authority (SAGIA), 15

Silent partner, 80, 100
Stock market-quoted companies, 87–88
Strategies, 36
Suitcase bankers, 82

T
Takeover targets, 88
Tax free, 67
Taxation, 66
Transaction cost, 74
Transfer risk, 46
True partnerships, 100
Turning East, 22–23

U
UK Briberies Act, 81, 100
US Foreign Corrupt Practices Act, 81, 100

V
Valuation gap, 90
Value determination, 89–91
Value-based consumption, 26–27

W
Western economies, 3
Wholly-owned subsidiaries, 76–80
Women, rise of, 20–22
World Association of Investment Promotion Agencies (WAIPA), 69
World Bank governance indicators, 56
World Economic Forum global competitiveness measures, 54
World Economic Forum, 53
World Trade Organization (WTO), 3, 15

Y
Yahoo, 93

Announcing the Business Expert Press Digital Library

Concise E-books Business Students Need for Classroom and Research

This book can also be purchased in an e-book collection by your library as

- a one-time purchase,
- that is owned forever,
- allows for simultaneous readers,
- has no restrictions on printing, and
- can be downloaded as PDFs from within the library community.

Our digital library collections are a great solution to beat the rising cost of textbooks. e-books can be loaded into their course management systems or onto student's e-book readers.

The **Business Expert Press** digital libraries are very affordable, with no obligation to buy in future years. For more information, please visit **www.businessexpertpress.com/librarians**. To set up a trial in the United States, please contact **Adam Chesler** at *adam.chesler@businessexpertpress .com* for all other regions, contact **Nicole Lee** at *nicole.lee@igroupnet.com.*

OTHER TITLES IN OUR INTERNATIONAL BUSINESS COLLECTION

Collection Editors: **Tamer Cavusgil, Michael Czinkota, and Gary Knight**

- *Export Marketing Strategy: Tactics and Skills that Work* by Tamer Cavusgil, Shaoming Zou, and Daekwan Kim
- *Born Global Firms: A New International Enterprise* by Gary Knight and Tamer Cavusgil
- *Conducting Market Research for International Business* by Tamer Cavusgil, Gary Knight, John Riesenberger, and Attila Yaprak
- *Emerging Trends, Threats and Opportunities in International Marketing: What Executives Need to Know* by Michael Czinkota, Ilkka Ronkainen, and Masaaki Kotabe
- *The Internationalists: Masters of the Global Game* by Catherine Scherer
- *Managing International Business in Relation-Based Versus Rule-Based Countries* by Shaomin Li
- *International Social Entrepreneurship* by Joseph Mark Munoz
- *Doing Business in the ASEAN Countries* by Balbir Bhasin
- *Successful Cross-Cultural Management: A Guidebook for International Managers* by Parissa Haghirian
- *Understanding Japanese Management Practices* by Parissa Hagihirian
- *A Strategic and Tactical Approach to Global Business Ethics* by Lawrence A. Beer

...ation can be obtained at www.ICGtesting.com
'SA
'9912

)004B/5/P